ORANGE

Nathan K. Bryce is the author of an extensive collection of books, training presentations, course materials, lesson plans, blogs, videos, and online resources which teach a variety of life-enriching, relationship-strengthening, success-building skills. In 1994, he invented and patented the Insight Personality Instrument™ which has been used by hundreds of thousands of people around the world to accurately identify their unique blend of temperaments. This book, and its three companion volumes, are based on this instrument and seek to teach the reader the positive strengths or virtues associated with each temperament. Adopting these admirable characteristics, attitudes, and behaviors will help anyone, regardless of personality type, find more happiness, success, and joy in their personal and professional lives.

ORANGE

Published by Four Lenses | PO Box 138 | Riverton UT 84065-0089
+1 877 745 1566

©2023 Nathan K. Bryce. All right reserved.

No part of this book may be reproduced or transmitted in any form by any means—graphic, electronic, or mechanical, including photocopying, recording, or by any information storage and retrieval system—without permission in writing from the author and publisher, except when permitted by law.

The author and publisher disclaim all warranties with regard to the suitability of this book in predicting or changing behavior. In no event shall the author and publisher be liable for any indirect, incidental, special, or consequential damages out of or in connection with the furnishing, performance, or use of this book.

First printed: May 2023

10   9   8   7   6   5   4   3   2   1

Printed in the United States of America

ISBN 979-8-9882167-0-4

CONTENTS

ADAPTABILITY — 1

Introduction | Handling life's challenges	2
Lesson 1 | Face challenges head-on	5
Lesson 2 | Get a handle on uncertainties	8
Lesson 3 | Identify creative solutions	12
Lesson 4 | Acquire necessary skills	16
Lesson 5 | Reinforce relationships	20
Lesson 6 | Reduce stress and tension	24

ADROITNESS — 29

Introduction | Showing finesse, agility, and grace	30
Lesson 1 | Sharpen your skills	32
Lesson 2 | Embrace agility	35
Lesson 3 | Show grace under pressure	38
Lesson 4 | Artfully help others	41
Lesson 5 | Practice social finesse	45
Lesson 6 | Lead through example	48

CANDOR 51
Introduction | How to cut to the chase 52
Lesson 1 | Speak truth freely 55
Lesson 2 | Seduce your audience 59
Lesson 3 | Lay down your weapons 62
Lesson 4 | Provide a remedy 66
Lesson 5 | Champion civility 69
Lesson 6 | Be aware of triggers 74

COURAGE 77
Introduction | Six steps to living a life full of courage 78
Lesson 1 | Show physical courage 81
Lesson 2 | Show moral courage 84
Lesson 3 | Show social courage 87
Lesson 4 | Show emotional courage 90
Lesson 5 | Show intellectual courage 94
Lesson 6 | Show spiritual courage 97

FREEDOM 101
Introduction | Choosing the freedoms that matter 102
Lesson 1 | Choose freely 105
Lesson 2 | Know your rights 109
Lesson 3 | Accept responsibilities 112
Lesson 4 | Evaluate consequences 116
Lesson 5 | Cherish freedom 120
Lesson 6 | Grant personal freedoms 123

IMMEDIACY 129
Introduction | How to enjoy immediacy 130
Lesson 1 | Master impulsivity 132
Lesson 2 | Get up close and personal 136
Lesson 3 | Control appetites 140
Lesson 4 | Listen to inner voice 144
Lesson 5 | Enhance your senses 147
Lesson 6 | Improvise your performance 151

IMPACT — 155
Introduction | Strategies for making a lasting impact — 156
Lesson 1 | Identify your friends — 158
Lesson 2 | Extend your influence — 162
Lesson 3 | Get stuff done — 167
Lesson 4 | Develop more charisma — 170
Lesson 5 | Make a colorful first impression — 174
Lesson 6 | Assess your impact — 178

INITIATIVE — 181
Introduction | Showing initiative — 182
Lesson 1 | Get out of your rut — 185
Lesson 2 | Work for yourself — 189
Lesson 3 | Tackle more tasks — 193
Lesson 4 | Seize the day — 197
Lesson 5 | Rock the boat — 201
Lesson 6 | Jump start others — 205

OPTIMISM   209

Introduction | How optimism beats pessimism   210
Lesson 1 | Measure your optimism   213
Lesson 2 | Take back control   217
Lesson 3 | Decrease negativity   221
Lesson 4 | Repeat aspirational affirmations   224
Lesson 5 | Choose gladness   231
Lesson 6 | Make promises to yourself   237

PERFORMANCE   241

Introduction | Stepping up your performance   242
Lesson 1 | Narrow your focus   245
Lesson 2 | Passionately deliver value   248
Lesson 3 | Prime your pump   251
Lesson 4 | Upgrade your thoughts   254
Lesson 5 | Make micro adjustments   258
Lesson 6 | Enjoy the flow   262

PERSUASIVENESS — 267
Introduction | How to convince anyone — 268
Lesson 1 | Learn Greek — 271
Lesson 2 | Target values — 275
Lesson 3 | Speak colorfully — 278
Lesson 4 | Watch your tone — 282
Lesson 5 | Engage everyone — 286
Lesson 6 | Avoid manipulation — 290

PLAYFULNESS — 295
Introduction | Why exhibiting playfulness helps — 296
Lesson 1 | Liberate your imagination — 298
Lesson 2 | Playfully explore — 301
Lesson 3 | Enjoy dizzying fun — 305
Lesson 4 | Ungag your humor — 308
Lesson 5 | Clown around — 311
Lesson 6 | Play colorfully — 315

VITALITY 319

Introduction | How to boost vitality and kill vampires	320
Lesson 1 | Measure your energy	323
Lesson 2 | Boost your energy	327
Lesson 3 | Avoid vampires	332
Lesson 4 | Demonstrate enthusiasm	336
Lesson 5 | Fire up your fascination	340
Lesson 6 | Make time for fun	344

Introduction

Handling life's challenges and uncertainties with adaptability

Have you ever known someone who is so stuck in their attitudes or behaviors that they are unwilling to change despite overwhelming reasons that they should change? Sometimes, individuals hold on to ideas and philosophies and skills that are way past their use-by date, like a bulging can of tomato sauce. If you don't mind consuming clostridium botulinum, a bacterium that can cause the disease known as botulism, and want to risk paralyzed muscles, difficulty speaking or swallowing, or blurred vision, then, heck it, go ahead and consume the contents of that bulging can. But I wouldn't. I would toss out that can and get a new one. Sometimes, our ideas, attitudes, and behaviors also need to be tossed out and replaced with something that won't kill our dreams or harm our relationships.

Adaptability is the ability to adjust easily and effectively to change. It is being open to modifying your attitudes and behaviors to meet the demands of the situation. It helps you shift gears without a lot of friction and resistance. It is being flexible, versatile, and resilient in the face of adversity or stress.

The first rule of adaptability is to face challenges head-on. In this reading assignment, we will learn how to become an emergency aid provider—someone who has the skills to be able to jump into the middle of a crisis, perform triage, and do whatever it takes to rescue and recover, regardless of whether it belongs in the physical, emotional, financial, intellectual, or social domain. We'll talk about what behaviors will help you become a highly adaptable first responder.

The second rule of adaptability is to get a handle on uncertainties. Uncertainty is difficult to live with even though it has become a hallmark of our society. We persistently worry about money, job security, housing, safety, relationships, health, and politics. It is no wonder so many of us suffer from anxiety disorders. If we learn how to properly identify the things we can control versus the things we can't, and spot the constancy that exists amidst change, then we can become more resilient and cope with our uncertainties.

The third rule of adaptability is to identify creative solutions. Adaptable individuals don't hesitate to take their toolbox and start working on solving immediate problems. The toolbox may not contain the specialized tools that could do the job better or faster, but it does contain a hammer for breaking things apart and some duct tape for putting things back together. Sometimes you've just got to MacGyver it and temporarily fix the problem until you have more resources to apply a permanent fix.

The fourth rule of adaptability is to acquire necessary skills. This includes both hard skills, like using tools appropriately, as well as soft skills, like communication, interpersonal, cognitive, and organizational skills. Do you know which skills you need to adapt to your changing world?

The fifth rule of adaptability is to reinforce relationships. The ability to cope with change is challenging to manage on your own. It can be done alone, and has been done alone, but it is far easier if you have a friend or family member who can help you through the necessary changes, who have your best interests at heart, and are willing to be there when you need them.

The sixth rule of adaptability is to reduce stress and tension. You may be aware that most people have a built-in, automatic response to stress and tension, such as whether or not to freeze in our tracks, flee the scene, or fight it out. Different scenarios require different responses. Do you know how to make sure you don't buckle under pressure and succumb to the weight of your challenges?

These six steps will help you develop the ability to solve problems and make decisions in high-pressure situations, when it is crucial that you adapt to the circumstances you are facing in positive, effective ways. We will learn when it is finally time to adapt and make changes to your life in order to reduce obstacles and make forward progress. I look forward to studying this virtue with you.

Lesson 1

Face challenges head-on

A serious automobile accident seems to come at us from nowhere in the blink of an eye. But in that instant, it shatters our plans, demolishes our mobility, severs our independence, and has the potential to wreck our lives. A quick call to emergency services sends a rescue vehicle or two and they rush on the scene to render aid. After securing the scene from causing further damage, the first responders triage the injuries of the people, which means they split the wounded into groups based on the seriousness of their injuries and then make decisions about the treatment the injured should be given according to the resources available and their chances of survival. This sorting process is essential to maximize the number of survivors.

Change is often as unexpected and unpredictable as a serious automobile accident. When change collides with our expectations and alters our plans, highly adaptable people are needed to jump in and perform triage and do whatever it takes to rescue and recover.

Regardless of the nature of the change, rescuers use their various skills to secure the scene so that innocent bystanders remain safe, identify those who have been injured, quickly assess the seriousness of injuries, and treat those who need urgent assistance before working on those who need less help. They may not possess all the required knowledge and skills, but the make the best with what they have and what they are able to do.

Dealing with significant changes, critical issues, and performing triage takes a plucky combination of composure, expertise, problem-solving, flexibility, compassion, and people skills. Normally, these courageous action figures are driven, competitive, passionate, and concerned with getting positive results—even if that means they need to do risky, improvised things.

Do you have what it takes to be the "go to" person when change smacks you in the face? Can you abandon whatever role you were performing before the crisis and step up to do whatever it required to do? Do you have the skills to handle emergencies, deal with disasters, and face critical issues? Here are a few behaviors that will help you become a highly adaptive first responder.

- Willing to assess dangers and face them head-on.
- Make appropriate decisions at critical times.
- Step up and take action during a crisis.
- Motivate others to help perform necessary tasks.
- Maintain composure and objectivity during emergencies.
- Navigate your way through tricky situations.
- Put the needs of others before your own.
- Focus and think clearly in times of urgency.
- Remain focused and determined during emergencies.
- Quickly determine how to use available resources.
- Set aside personal feelings to handle important tasks.

"Men ever follow willingly a daring leader: most willingly of all, in great emergencies."

—Robert Dale Owen

Assignments

🖉 1A: What are some of the more memorable changes you have had to face in the past? Explain how you adapted or didn't adapt to those changes.

🖉 1B: Have you ever been rescued by another person, either physically, emotionally, financially, intellectually, or socially? Describe the admirable behaviors of that person.

🖉 1C: What are some ways you can improve your adaptability?

🖉 1D: Describe a change that needs to be made in your life and how you plan to adapt to it.

Lesson 2

Get a handle on uncertainties

For most people, uncertainty is difficult to live with even though it has become a hallmark of our society. We persistently worry about money, job security, housing, safety, relationships, health, and politics. Anxiety disorders are now the most common mental illness in the world, with nearly 1 out of 5 people suffering from its affects, often using legal and illegal substances to relieve their symptoms. Many are also diagnosed with obsessive-compulsive disorder, depression, post-traumatic stress disorders, or eating disorders. If you have a need for most things to be "black and white", become frustrated when things are unpredictable, only perform your best in stable situations and environments, or fear how you will fare if things go badly, then it may be helpful for you to acquire a bit more flexibility.

> "Uncertainty is the only certainty there is, and knowing how to live with insecurity is the only security."
>
> —John Allen Paulos

A flexible attitude allows you to look at the things that are uncertain around you while simultaneously evaluating the things that are not going to change. It helps to make a list of those uncertain things so you know exactly what you are worried about. Spend some time with this list and make it as thorough as you can. Now go back and cross out the items you cannot control, because there is nothing you can do about it. You should be left with a list of reasonable worries that are within your ability to control.

Next, make another list of the things that are more certain, that aren't likely to change, like governments over-taxing its citizens. Of course, we know that everything could change because that is the nature of people, places, things, theories, and facts, but some things are not likely to change any time soon. For instance, if you love your children, that love is not likely to change even when they start acting in bone-headed ways. Or perhaps you love a particular athletic team, even though players and managers come and go, you still are willing to support them, watch their games, and buy their merchandise. Again, cross out the things you can't control, leaving a list of things that you can influence.

Spotting constancy amidst change is helpful and helps keep things in perspective. Enjoy the assurance and stability it provides. Then turn to your list of worries and courageously face the items that you can control. To help you do that, consider adopting some of the characteristics or behaviors of those who can adapt and handle the uncertainties in their lives:

- Identify the things that are changing and those that are remaining the same.
- Easily respond to changing conditions.
- Limit exposure to bad news or argumentative commentary.
- Don't try to make sense of things too soon.
- Invite others to help you find solutions.
- Receive support from trusted friends and family members.
- Readily change gears whenever something unexpected happens.
- Reflect on past successes rather than failures.
- Take the future one day at a time.
- Let go of things that can't be controlled.
- Envision the best rather than the worst.

- Adjust plans to changing conditions.
- Perform well in uncertain situations.
- Know when to quit for the day.
- Adapt attitudes and behaviors to changing situations.
- Commit to gradually face uncertainty rather than avoiding it.
- Focus on the things that give your life meaning.
- Don't underestimate your ability to cope with challenges.
- Accept that absolute certainty is an impossible fantasy.

Assignments

✐ 2A: What do you do to avoid facing uncertainty?

✐ 2B: What are some "self-care" things you can do to develop more resilience?

✐ 2C: What is one thing that has recently changed in your life that you found difficult to cope with? With what you have learned so far, what can you do to better cope with it?

Lesson 3

Identify creative solutions

Adaptable individuals don't hesitate to take their toolbox and start working on solving immediate problems. The toolbox may not contain the specialized tools that could do the job better or faster, but it does contain a hammer for breaking things apart and some duct tape for putting things back together. Sometimes you've just got to MacGyver it and temporarily fix the problem until you have more resources to apply a permanent fix. It may not be pretty, but it is functional and practical. All it takes is a little out-of-the-box thinking coupled with a healthy dose of creativity and a few paper clips to improvise solutions.

> "MacGyver (pronounced \muh-GHYE-ver\) is a verb that means to make or repair with what is on hand; to assemble or repair something by ingenious improvisation using everyday items that would not usually be used for the purpose."
>
> —Merriam-Webster Online Dictionary

Adaptable people are also known for their ability to adapt or modify things into other things, often in creative and practical ways. When you need to get the dust out of your couch cushions, grab your old tennis racket and beat away on a windy day.

If you need to label your cords before you plug them into a packed power strip, write the name of the device on the plastic tab from a bread loaf bag and push it onto the cord. Do you want to save plastic shopping bags for later use? Stuff them into an old paper towel tube. When your shoes are muddy, but you need to run indoors for a moment, insert each foot into one of those plastic bags and tie it around your ankles. Want to start some seeds in the spring? Poke some holes into a plastic clamshell container, fill it with potting soil, insert the seeds, spritz it with water, and place it in a sunny spot. Need to clean your computer monitor or TV screen? Use a coffee filter.

Creative solutions expand to the workplace. Rather than having a sit-down meeting, have a stand-up meeting—it will accelerate the tempo. Change up your routines by turning off your autopilot and doing them in different ways—you may find a better way to get the job done. Rather than explaining your thoughts to others, draw a picture or a diagram—a bad drawing is better than no drawing. Introduce a random thing into your day to help you think outside your box, like counting the number of steps it takes to walk to a certain point, wearing something unexpected, telling a new joke, or when someone asks, "how are you?" giving them a clever retort. Shake things up a bit to help jump-start your creativity.

Here are some of the behaviors of creative and flexible thinkers:

- Use whatever resources are on hand to solve the problem.
- Be open to new experiences and new perspectives.
- Admit when you are wrong and make corrections as needed.
- Look at problems from many different angles.
- Play with various ideas until you find the right one.
- Explore connections between seemingly unrelated items.
- Shake up routines and patterns.
- Be willing to hear and test out new ideas.

- Refrain from judging the ideas of others too quickly.
- Explore fascinating and interesting things.
- Use different materials, ingredients, or processes.
- Have fun in the process and don't take it too seriously.
- Develop unique ways of analyzing complex problems.
- Don't pressure yourself to get it right the first time.
- Encourage others to approach you with new ideas.
- Take calculated risks and push the limits.

Assignments

- 3A: Describe someone, real or imaginary, who seems to be able to adapt to whatever life throws at them. What makes them adaptable?

- 3B: What prevents people from being adaptable?

- 3C: What can be done to help people become more adaptable?

- 3D: What is the most creative solution you have developed to solve a problem in your life?

- 3E: What problem are you currently facing that could benefit from an out-of-the-box solution?

- 3F: Read articles, reports, or books written by people who have an opposing viewpoint. For example, if you are politically conservative, read some radically progressive literature. As you read, practice your empathy skills and try to think about and understand the person's beliefs, values, and motives.

Lesson 4

Acquire necessary skills

Adaptability is the ability to rapidly learn what needs to be done in changing circumstances and then use those skills and behaviors to face your challenges. Sometimes these "hard skills" focus on using a particular software program, operating a piece of heavy machinery, diagnosing medical problems, or fixing the transmission on an automobile. These skills are usually acquired through some sort of educational process or training regimen. Because of your familiarity with one tool, when its replacement comes along, hopefully you can quickly understand the changes and adapt to the new equipment or procedure.

> "For organisations, flexibility is a must to cope with fluctuations in demand and remain competitive, and people must be able to develop adaptable attitudes to quickly embrace evolving business conditions, new business opportunities, and shifting strategies."
>
> —Alain Dehaze

There are also "soft skills" that affect your ability to adapt to the changes around you. Some of these have been taught to you, some of them stem from your natural instincts or personality style, but others require you to spend some effort learning them on your own. What are these soft skills? There are four general categories: communication, interpersonal, cognitive, and organizational skills.

Communication skills allow you to gather, interpret, and disseminate information. Learning to write well, read well, speak well, listen well, and use body language and facial expressions in intentional ways, helps you learn or teach others what needs to be done to cope with change. To do that effectively, you need to pay close attention to those with whom you're communicating, engaging them by asking questions and clarifying ideas, rephrasing, or restating until the message is clearly understood and acknowledged.

Interpersonal skills such as honesty, teamwork, patience, dependability, and compromise are essential whenever you work with others. They also give you a chance to demonstrate confidence, friendliness, empathy, and respect. Understanding human temperament is a crucial interpersonal skill, allowing you to understand what people value, what strengths they naturally possess, what motivates them, how to interact in meaningful ways, and how to avoid things that cause stress and frustration.

Cognitive skills include the ability to research the cause of the problem, analyze the situation, ask questions, make observations, form connections, review past solutions, and if necessary, develop new strategies. They problem-solving skills take advantage of your creative and experimental abilities and use them in powerful and efficient ways.

Organizational skills include managing time, keeping the channels of communication open, delegating responsibilities, reporting progress, paying attention to details, staying focused, developing step-by-step objectives to reach goals, making necessary course corrections, and keeping proper perspective of the entire process.

People who have developed the requisite hard and soft skills to roll with the punches, are often identified by the following characteristics:

- Are confident in abilities but are open to improvement.
- Explore new approaches for getting things done.
- Ask others to help them learn new skills.
- Take personal responsibility for acquiring new skills.
- Quickly learn new methods to solve problems.
- Practice new skills intentionally and regularly.
- Keep skills and knowledge current and applicable.
- Commit to continually learn new skills before they are needed.
- Take action to improve performance deficiencies.
- Not threatened by the opinions of others.

Assignments

🖉 4A: What additional skills will help you become more adaptive?

🖉 4B: Do you know someone who was not able to cope with changes to their world? What skills were they lacking?

🖉 4C: What skills are you lacking?

🖉 4D: What is your plan to acquire the skills you need?

🖉 4E: Do something that is breaks away from your normal routines and is completely uncharacteristic of your dominant temperament. For example, if you're primarily Gold, perhaps you can go somewhere on a whim (Orange), keep a diary of your thoughts and feelings (Blue), or play a game of chess (Green).

Lesson 5

Reinforce relationships

When making changes in your own life, such as dropping a particularly addictive habit, starting a new job, learning a new skill, or moving to different locale, the ability to cope with change is challenging to manage on your own. It can be done alone, and has been done alone, but it is far easier if you have a friend or family member who can help you through the necessary changes, who have your best interests at heart, and are willing to be there when you need them. Even if the only thing they do is empathetically listen while you express your feelings and talk about your struggles, this selfless service will help maintain your emotional balance and keep you connected to the things that matter most. Most of us, including the most introverted introvert, are social beings who tend to lose our way when we feel alone or isolated. We truly need each other to survive and thrive.

> "The key thing is knowing how to adapt. Adapting to the group that you have at your disposal; adapting to the place where you're working; adapting to the local environment. This is crucial: adaptability."
>
> —Didier Deschamps

Maintaining relationships is a high priority for those who can adapt and make changes in their lives. They need people around to help them through the rough patches of life. However, relationships are dynamic things that are seldom set in cement. Is your best friend at age eight still your best friend today? Do you still have a crush on your first love interest? Is a former spouse still the apple of your eye? Are you as close to your brothers or sisters as when you shared the same home? Our relationships, like a campfire, will go out unless continually watched over and fed additional fuel and oxygen. Even though our relationships burn bright and provide heat tonight, tomorrow they will be cold and dead if we don't take care. Breathing life into the relationships you want to keep is a constant need and should receive a good deal of our attention. Quality time is not sufficient to make up for a lack of quantity—both are required.

When facing changes that involve multiple people, such as a company merger, economic downturns, emergencies, or natural disasters, adaptability isn't an optional characteristic—it is crucial attribute. When times are tough, everyone needs to figure out new ways of working together to achieve common goals, regardless of their diverse backgrounds, cultures, or experiences. That means people need to be willing to work side-by-side as they shoulder new responsibilities and carry new burdens. Even if you have developed expertise in a particular area, you may need to let someone else do that job while you do another. They will likely need help doing it successfully just like you need help doing your new job successfully. To do that requires a healthy, reciprocating relationship, where trust, patience, and friendliness are present in every interaction. Everyone needs to be on their best behavior and ditch all the idiosyncrasies and imperfections that harm relationships. In time, the crisis will be resolved, the weather will calm down, the virus will die out, the destruction will end, and those left standing will return to a new normal life, but one where relationships are valued even more than they were before.

Here are a few characteristics of flexible individuals who appreciate the need for strong and healthy relationships while making necessary changes in their lives:

- Are open-minded to new approaches or new solutions.
- Are cooperative and compromising when dealing with others.
- Enjoy the variety and learning experiences that come from working with people of different backgrounds.
- Believe it is important to be flexible when dealing with others.
- Enjoy learning about cultures other than their own.
- Perceive the strengths of others and use that knowledge in interactions.
- Show respect for the culture and heritage of others.
- Feel comfortable interacting with others who have different values and customs.
- Work effectively with others regardless of similarities or differences.
- Can relate to others and understand how they are feeling at any moment.
- Adapt behavior to get along with others.

Assignments

✎ 5A: Think of a relationship that is currently dying in your life. What will you lose when it is gone?

✎ 5B: How have people helped you in the past adapt and deal with difficult changes?

✎ 5C: How do people know that you have their back and can be relied on to help them anytime?

✎ 5D: What can you do to strengthen the important relationships in your life?

✎ 5E: Find someone who has a reputation for being adaptable and let them be your mentor. Carefully observe their attitudes and behaviors for a while. Keep notes on what they do, and don't do. Then, as soon as you can, start emulating those behaviors. Ask your mentor for feedback and, if needed, a pep talk. Keep on practicing until you feel confident and begin to experience success.

Lesson 6

Reduce stress and tension

When you walk into a very cold room your brain instantaneously receives input from your body's sensory nerves warning it about a potential danger to your health and survival. To handle the stress and keep your inner temperature from dropping too low, your brain automatically activates its thermoregulation routine and sends signals to the glands of your skin to generate some "goose bumps" to pull your body hair upright to insulate you from further heat loss—which is only helpful if you have a particularly furry coat of skin. Your brain also sends signals to your muscles and organs to start vigorously vibrating to produce heat—we call it shivering. It also slows down other processes to conserve energy, like your nervous system and blood flow, which is why your extremities feel colder faster and are the first to grow numb. If these coping mechanisms are successful before you have a chance to leave the room, you live; if not, you find out for yourself if there is life after death.

> "Stress is the inability to adapt to a changing environment."
>
> —Malcolm John Rebennack

Most of the stress we feel as we go about our lives is managed in the same way as our brain automatically triggers responses to either freeze, flee, or fight. Most of the time these responses are beyond our control. We each have our own unique range of stress we can take before we need to get our keisters of Dodge City. Highly adaptable people seem to have a wider range then the rest of us, partly because of their positive, confident attitudes and the vast arsenal of skills at their disposal. This allows them to deftly handle a variety of stressful circumstances like a hemophiliac who is confidently juggling razor-sharp daggers.

Adaptable people are adaptable because they don't buckle under pressure. They play the hand they have been dealt, rather than scooping up their chips and backing away from the table. Their optimistic demeanor, even if it is a bluff, allows them to carry on regardless of wins and losses. The courage to keep moving forward, despite challenging changes, is often contagious. As it spreads to others, it tends to calm things down, de-escalate tensions, and eliminate pain points—which helps others get their head back into the game.

Here are some additional characteristics of individuals who are cognitively, emotionally, and dispositionally flexible enough to handle the stress that accompanies change:

- Determine how well they are adapting to the change.
- Can work even in uncomfortable or unpleasant environments.
- Adept at using their skills to complete relevant tasks.
- Remain capable even when their schedule is too full.
- Feel equipped to deal with stress and conflict.
- Work effectively even when tired or exhausted.
- Don't get overwhelmed when assigned a large workload.
- Adopt active coping styles and implement problem-focused coping strategies.
- Push themselves to complete important tasks.
- Identify positive reactions to difficult circumstances.
- Maintain a cheery, upbeat disposition despite setbacks.
- Select relevant and appropriate strategies for any situation.

- Maintain a good-natured attitude when under a great deal of stress.
- Regulate their behavior to change or create the change in the situation.
- Acquire the appropriate knowledge about the situation and how they are performing in it.
- Rarely over-react to stressful or difficult news.

Assignments

- 6A: Have you ever been so stressed-out that you couldn't do your job? Explain how that felt.

- 6B: What events regularly trigger a stress response in your life?

- 6C: What signs do you see in your mind or body that you are under stress?

- 6D: What can you do to be more prepared when stress strikes you in the future?

- 6E: Practice solving problems and making decisions in high-pressure situations. For example, if you have trouble thinking when things are noisy and chaotic, try making decisions someplace that is noisy and chaotic, like a crowded restaurant, a busy airport, or a packed sports stadium. Keep doing this until you can focus on the problem and tune out the distractions. Then start to reduce the amount of time you give yourself to come up with a solution.

Introduction

Showing finesse, agility, grace, and adroitness

Adroitness. It comes the French word "adroit" which was first used in the 1600s. It isn't used very often nowadays. Essentially it means you have the capacity to do things with your mind or body that makes you stand out from others. Whether you inherited a specific talent or ability or simply worked your tail off at something until you became an expert at it, the result is the same: pure poetry in motion.

Adroitness is being expert or nimble in the use of the hands or body. You give a graceful and skillful performance. You have the ability to operate something, such as a piece of equipment or machinery, without difficulty-you make the complicated look simple. You're physically coordinated, agile, and dexterous.

Here are the six things we'll be focusing on in the reading and assignments for this virtue.

First, we will learn to sharpen our skills so that we can do intricate or precise tasks without thinking too much about it. Muscle memory takes over become you have sharpened and honed your skills.

Second, we will try to embrace agility. This means you are nimble, spry, alert, frisky, active, flexible, and responsive. These characteristics don't just apply to your physical abilities, but your mental abilities as well.

Next, we will attempt to show grace under pressure. Gracefulness is the quality of having or showing balance, elegance, and poise in private or in public, in peaceful or tumultuous times.

Fourth, we will artfully help others. This means you allow your native creativity and cleverness to devise schemes and strategies that promote positive attitudes and behaviors.

Fifth, we will practice social finesse. This means you have a chameleon-like ability to fit into just about any social situation, temporarily setting aside your own preferences for the sake of getting along with others.

Finally, we will try to lead through example. If you are adroit, you are willing to take a stand and lead out, both physically and morally. It also means that you had developed the skill to show others through example how to do things excellently.

Now that you know what I means when I use the word "adroitness," are you ready to work on it with me? Are you up to the challenge to achieve excellence? Let get moving.

Lesson 1

Sharpen your skills

Adroit people have the capacity to do things with their mind or body that make them stand out from others. Whether they inherited a specific talent or ability or simply worked their tail off at something until they became an expert at it, the result is the same: pure poetry in motion. It is a pleasure to watch them work because they make the difficult seem so easy.

"No tricks, no tools, but talent makes a task truly top class."

—Amit Kalantri

An adroit person has dexterity. This term is often used to describe someone who can use their hands to do intricate tasks. But it is much more than the ability to quickly move your fingers into various positions so that you can play games, compose messages, write software, paint masterpieces, whittle sticks, sew stitches, twirl pencils, tie shoes, floss teeth, use chopsticks, make shadow puppets, or express rude gestures. Dexterity also refers to the physical and mental skills or techniques you have acquired that allow you to deftly perform any task without thinking about it too much. Your body's muscle memory takes over because you have sharpened and honed your skills as sharp as possible. Similarly, mental dexterity means that you have disciplined your mind and can think of quick or creative solutions to problems.

If you want to become adroit at something, you first need to choose something that you don't mind doing today, tomorrow, the next day, and perhaps the rest of your life. If you could do one thing exceptionally well, what would that one thing be? Make that your goal and start investing the time and energy to become proficient at it. Once you grasp it and have mastered the fundamentals, then kick it up a notch and turn your performance into a certifiable masterpiece. It should become so instinctive and automatic that it doesn't require much effort to execute. It becomes an integral part of your identity, like golfing is to Tiger Woods, making deals is to Donald Trump, hockey is to Wayne Gretzky, basketball is to Michael Jordan, investing is to Warren Buffet, nonviolent resistance is to Gandhi, and so on.

Assignments

🖉 1A: What are 10 skills that you wish you had? Can you think of an activity that incorporates a number of those skills? Which skill is your top priority?

🖉 1B: List some famous people who already possess the skills you want to acquire. Do you know anyone locally who is good at that skill too? Find out if they would be willing to mentor you on your journey.

Lesson 2

Embrace agility

An adroit person is agile, which means they are nimble, spry, alert, frisky, active, flexible, and responsive. These characteristics don't just apply to their physical abilities, but their mental abilities as well. They are great observers of the world around them and are constantly gathering information that might affect their next actions. Like a secret agent in a spy movie, they want to be able to get up and go in a moment's notice. They don't like sitting with their back to people, and prefer to be situated where they can see as much as possible without being boxed in.

In the corporate world, agility is the ability to respond quickly to changes and get the competitive upper hand. As markets change, an agile employee can swiftly move to a different role or team and assume new responsibilities. If you have an agile structure, then you have an iterative approach to managing projects where your team can deliver value to your customers faster than your competitors.

> "Success today requires the agility and drive to constantly rethink, reinvigorate, react, and reinvent."
> —Bill Gates

Agility gives you the freedom to move quickly, easily, and accurately. You aren't married to the traditional status quo and embrace improvements and innovations. You are on the lookout for information that moves the ball towards the goal post, even if it contradicts preconceived notions. You cut through any unnecessary work and bureaucracy so you can focus on the essentials. If that means you need to stand out, find shortcuts, or take risks, then you are up to the challenge.

Because of their ability to adjust on the fly, agile people are constantly sorting through the list of things they need to do and shifting priorities as needed. Whenever a new task comes their way, they evaluate it into four buckets of diminishing priority: what tasks must be done if the project is to succeed, what tasks should be done, what tasks could be done if they had enough resources to work on it, and what tasks won't be done because they aren't required. After the tasks in the first bucket are completed, they will then move on to the second bucket, and so forth.

Assignments

✏ 2A: What do you already do that shows agility?

✏ 2B: What is preventing you from being more agile?

✏ 2C: What can you do to be more agile?

Lesson 3

Show grace under pressure

When most people think of gracefulness, they often think of a swan or a ballet dancer. But it also applies to the welder who walks along a solitary beam at the top of a burgeoning skyscraper. You see it in sports whenever a player does a complicated routine or a highly technical maneuver that almost takes your breath away. It appears in courtrooms as attorneys present and argue over evidence. You see it in a championship boxing ring as opponents float like a butterfly and sting like a bee. You hear it in a concert when instrumentalists, singers, and crew members work in complete harmony to deliver a spectacular performance. If you are seeing someone do something with out-of-the-ordinary physicality, skill, and finesse, you are seeing gracefulness.

> "Grace has been defined as the outward expression of the inward harmony of the soul."
>
> —William Hazlitt

Gracefulness is the quality of having or showing balance, elegance, and poise in private or in public, in peaceful or tumultuous times. Graceful people deal with pressures, obstacles, troubles, and trials without breaking their stride. In fact, they almost thrive on the extra energy required to deliver a good performance when everything else is falling apart. They have what it takes to keep it together and look extremely good while doing it.

Gracefulness also manifests itself in how we treat other people. If we are abrupt, surly, impolite, vulgar, snippy, rude, or disrespectful, we aren't being graceful. A graceful person will be as polished and gracious as the circumstances dictate. For example, at a formal event, they will be suave and sophisticated, being pleasant and charming in their conversations. When hanging out with friends after a hard day's work, where everyone is expected to cut loose and relax, a graceful person still treats others better than they deserve. They give others the benefit of the doubt and quickly forgive offenses.

Assignments

🖉 3A: Think of the most graceful person in your circle of acquaintances. What makes them graceful?

🖉 3B: In which situations or circumstances do you feel the most ungraceful or awkward?

🖉 3C: What can you do to show more gracefulness?

🖉 3D: How do you prefer to extend grace to others?

Lesson 4

Artfully help others

One of the definitions of adroitness includes the idea of "artfulness." Artfulness describes a person who takes unfair advantage of other people or is disingenuous or deceitful. Certainly, that could describe someone who has a relatively low amount of maturity in artfulness, but the highly mature artful person is cunning or crafty in a good way. They allow their native creativity and cleverness to devise schemes and strategies that promote positive attitudes and behaviors.

> "The smart way to keep people passive and obedient is to strictly limit the spectrum of acceptable opinion, but allow very lively debate within that spectrum—even encourage the more critical and dissident views. That gives people the sense that there's free thinking going on, while all the time the presuppositions of the system are being reinforced by the limits put on the range of the debate."
>
> —Noam Chomsky

For example, in the workplace, an artful Orange may promote shortening the workweek, having more enjoyable interactions with others, making the workplace more fun and interactive, giving higher rewards to higher achievers, spending energy on things that matter the most, getting rid of unnecessary paperwork and procedures, providing challenging assignments that require skill, gamifying performance, giving people a voice in the decisions that affect their lives, promoting flexibility and adaptability, and encouraging out-of-office activities. Notice that all of these outcomes clearly reflect Orange preferences, but they also appeal to just about every other temperament as well because they make work less tedious and more rewarding.

What makes it especially artful, is if they figure out ways to carefully lead others to "freely arrive" at a desired conclusion. The Overton Window, named after American policy analyst Joseph Overton, it an example of this artfulness. In essence, this strategy encourages you to offer someone choices: the first is too extreme in one direction, the second is somewhere in the middle, and the third is too extreme in the other direction. Even though you passionately argue for one or both extremes, you secretly hope that they choose the middle choice. They see it as a sensible compromise on your part, when in fact, it is what you wanted all along. You simply pushed them in the direction you wanted them to go. This tactic has been artfully used for decades by politicians, think tanks, and the media to move people out of their comfort zones towards a new normal.

In the case of the artful Orange above, if they wanted to promote a shorter workweek, they could design an Overton Window and present these options: have people work three 14-hour days each week, four 10-hour days each week, or reduce the required hours to 32 hours each week. They would argue most strongly for the first or last option while silently hoping for the middle option. Furthermore, they let those they are trying to persuade come up with their own reasons why the middle option would be the best option, such as saving fuel or time commuting.

Using persuasive techniques like the Overton Window is but one of the weapons in the arsenal of an artful tactician. Whether the weapons are used for good or bad purposes—that is up to the user. Certainly, you can them to pick the pockets of pedestrians like the Artful Dodger in Oliver Twist or seize control of a nation, but you can also use it to meaningfully motivate those who can't see how to rise up and achieve their dreams. For an emotionally mature person, artful techniques should always be used to help others rather than to help themselves.

Assignments

✏ 4A: Give an example of how someone has used the Overton Window to coerce you into doing something that you wouldn't have considered before.

✏ 4B: Describe some artful or creative techniques you could use to convince people to do something.

Lesson 5

Practice social finesse

Social finesse is one of the facets of adroitness. You have a chameleon-like ability to change the way you act to satisfy a particular requirement. In fact, you can quickly work your way into a favorable position within most social groups. Sometimes this means you pretend to enjoy things when, in fact, you dislike them. To do that you have to hold your opinions and feelings in check to make sure they don't interfere with your goals. You are temporarily setting aside your own preferences for the sake of getting along with others.

> "Finesse is the best adaptation of means to circumstances."
>
> —Thomas B. Macaulay

Like most virtues, this ability has a positive side and a negative side. When it is used to manipulate or deceive people for personal pleasure or amusement, or deployed to inflict harm or create havoc, then it is largely narcissistic or even psychopathic. But when used in its positive form, where you are genuinely interested into fitting into a group not for what they can do for you, but for what you can do for them, then it is generally accepted. Most of the world's politicians and influencers regularly use social finesse to delicately gather and carefully retain followers.

How do you know if you've crossed the line from finesse into manipulation? A manipulator will:

- Say things that they have no intention of doing.

- Refuse to take responsibility for their actions.
- Frequently blame, complain, and shame others.
- Prey on the conscientiousness or good nature of others.
- Play the role of the victim.
- Talk about others behind their backs.
- Encourage and promote disharmony, confusion, or intrigue.
- Hide behind carefully constructed facades.
- Ignore the boundaries of other people.
- Twist your words into something you don't recognize.

To be successful at social finesse, you need to be as authentic as possible. Just like most wolves fail at pretending to be sheep, most liars and cheats eventually get exposed. If you have a pair of wings, it is far better to join a flock of flying flamingos then it is to join a pride of ravenous lions. Seek out people and groups that align with your values and who share common interests and behaviors, and you will find it far easier, safer, and more enjoyable to fit in and get along.

Assignments

- 5A: An adroit person handles social interactions with finesse and skill. Identify some online videos that will help you acquire more expertise in this area.

- 5B: What social skills do you need to acquire or polish? Ask a loved one for their input.

Lesson 6

Lead through example

The French word "adroit" was first used in the 1600s. It meant that you have a trained hand and possess the ability to move or direct things forward. If you are adroit, you are willing to take a stand and lead out, both physically and morally. It also means that you had developed the skill to show others through example how to do things excellently. It is this facet of adroitness—leadership by example—that we will look at next.

> "A leader leads by example not by force."
>
> —Sun Tzu

The world has no shortage of people who think they are good leaders and aspire to tell others what to do. Most fail at leadership because they demand that others follow their desires or adopt their values. Imposing your will on someone else might lead to short-term gains at their expense, but ultimately ends in long-term failure for everyone. You simply can't force anyone to do anything without restricting or taking away their freedom to think and act for themselves—the favored tool of dastardly despots, dictators, demagogues, and demons. On the other hand, if you lead by example, by practicing what you preach, by showing others the benefits that come from your way of thinking, by making yourself worthy of following or emulating, by letting people willingly choose to follow you—that's when you become a true leader with followers who stay beside you on the journey to your goals.

Adroitness makes this look easy because you have already put forth the effort to become exceptional at what you do. You lead not for the glory of leading, but because you have "been there and done that" and know, through experience, what to watch out for and what needs to be done. You lead because you have amassed the familiarity, skills, talents, disciplines, and training that are required for a good performance. In fact, you are constantly honing those abilities to make sure you don't lag behind and lapse into lethargic limpness.

While you are quite capable of doing things yourself, this doesn't necessarily mean that you do it or always have all the answers to all the problems. Rather, you know how to delegate and how to marshal your troops to tackle the challenges. You don't have to be the expert in all things, you just need to be expert at knowing how to get the best out of your people. An adroit leader can assemble the nuts, bolts, and gears of an organizational machine and keep it operational and well-lubricated because they know what needs to be done and how to get it done as quickly as possible.

Assignments

✏ 6A: Describe a leader in your life who primarily led through example? How do you feel about that person?

✏ 6B: In your opinion, what are the characteristics of a great leader? Identify someone who possess a lot of those characteristics.

✏ 6C: Each temperament has a set of strengths that they bring to the table as leaders. What are the leadership strengths of your primary color?

Introduction

How to cut to the chase and speak with candor

Have you noticed how some people seem to beat-around-the-bush and never quite get to the point? They hem and haw and talk about everything except for the difficult issue that is on their mind—they talk about everything except for the elephant stomping around the room. On the other hand, have you met someone who knows how to cut-to-the-chase and courageously say what needs to be said, even if it means they risk sounding offensive? There aren't too many people out there who can do this and look cool doing it. The ability to speak truthfully, directly, and with frankness is what we call candor.

 Candor is the quality of being frank, blunt, and open when communicating with other people. You are ready and willing to talk candidly about what's on your mind. You don't evade difficult or unpleasant issues. You may use speech that is sometimes colorful and unorthodox.

In the reading assignments, we will focus on six steps that will help you be more candid.

First, we'll learn why it is necessary to speak truth freely. Sadly, this liberty is being increasingly throttled, especially if your opinion differs from the majority. This is why some people avoid speaking out. So how can we create a genuine "safe space" environment where people have the freedom to express their ideas without fear of rejection, retaliation, or retribution. We'll think about this for a bit.

Second, we'll learn how to seduce your audience. This is the art of attracting someone to your point-of-view. You appear to have some sort of inherent force or magnetic power to allure and charm others to your way of thinking. But it is more than this: it is serving up your information in attractive and appealing ways. We intentionally use language that speaks to the values and preferences of your audience.

Third, we will discover why we need to lay down our weapons. Candor can be used as a weapon, especially when used to threaten or intimidate, condemn or castigate, manipulate or malign, and embarrass or harass. If we're using it for those results, shame on us. Truth should never hurt—it should bring light and understanding and chase away confusion and uncertainty.

Fourth, we will try to provide a remedy. Most people can easily point out problems, but only a few are able to provide remedies that solve those problems. A candid person is willing to engage in open and honest give and take so that problems can be solved quickly. It is reciprocal in nature. If you only give out negative feedback, but never ask for it, you aren't being candid, you're being a bully.

Fifth, we will learn how to champion civility. Being open and direct doesn't give us license to be rude or offensive. At first glance, candor and civility seem to be opposite notions. If we define candor as being honest, genuine, forth-right, straightforward, and sincere, and define civility as being respectful, courteous, polite, gracious, cordial, and pleasant, is it possible to be both at the same time? Absolutely! They aren't antonyms at all.

Finally, we will show that we are aware of triggers that tend to make the problem worse, derail conversations, or tear people down. Being triggered is far more than just feeling uncomfortable or offended when someone isn't politically correct-it usually leads to a distressing, anxious mental state where an individual loses control of thoughts and emotions. The reading will delve into this in more detail.

So that's the game plan for how we're going to tackle this virtue. If we do those six things, we will not only be more candid, but we will be more helpful to others because we aren't wasting their time. In fact, we could say that being candid is really the polite thing to do. It shows that we care about and respect others by getting right to the point.

Lesson 1

Speak truth freely

2500 years ago, a fundamental component of classical Athenian democracy was the freedom of speech, where you could discuss just about anything without fear of punishment, including the taboo topics of politics and religion. The only caveat was you had to speak the truth and not intentionally lie, slander, or deceive people. This freedom was called *parrhesia,* which means "to speak everything" or "to speak freely with boldness." Of course, if you said something that didn't reflect the moral beliefs of the majority and was deemed untruthful or dangerous to society, it didn't end so well, especially for out-of-the-box thinkers like Socrates. To speak the truth required courage and commitment to your ideals because you were also putting your life at risk if you offended too many people.

> "Candor is the key to collaborating effectively. Lack of candor leads to dysfunctional environments."
>
> —Edwin Catmull

Today, being candid and frank is still an option for many people in the world. However, in some places, this liberty is being increasingly throttled, especially if your opinion differs from the majority. This is one of the reasons democracies don't work out very well for minorities and non-conformists, and one of the reasons why the founders of the United States of America abandoned democracy as a preferred form of government in favor of a constitutional federal republic where the people elect representatives to run their government. Historically speaking, in a majority-rules democracy, minorities are initially embraced, then tolerated, then ignored, then squashed as they become pests.

The previous paragraph is an example of candid frankness. Some people may disagree with it, which is their prerogative. While it provides factual information, those facts are subject to different interpretations and may elicit positive or negative reactions, especially if someone is highly passionate about their politics. Speech only becomes offensive if the speaker is trying to be offensive or if the listener chooses to be offended by it. Frankly, choosing not to be offended by the spoken or written word is a clear sign of emotional and intellectual maturity. It establishes a "safe space" environment where people have the freedom to express their ideas without fear of rejection, retaliation, or retribution.

What does candid behavior look like? If you are candid, you:

- Feel comfortable communicating with other people.
- Are willing to talk about what's on your mind.
- Don't dodge difficult or unpleasant issues.
- Use language that is sometimes colorful or unorthodox but not offensive.
- Express your views directly to each other without interruption or interference.
- Attempt to articulate what you are feeling and experiencing.
- Objectively evaluate and consider multiple perspectives.
- Mean what you say and say what you mean.
- Stick to the facts as much as possible.
- Never attack someone's character or values.
- Give both positive and negative feedback.
- Remain transparent and free from disguise or subterfuge.
- Aren't self-serving but trying to help others.

- Look beyond your own emotions and agenda.
- Avoid lies or deceit of any degree, even little white lies.
- Never communicate if you aren't in control of your emotions.

Assignments

🖉 1A: Can you be too candid? Explain.

🖉 1B: Why do some people avoid being candid?

🖉 1C: What can you do to establish a climate of candor in your relationships at home and at work?

Lesson 2

Seduce your audience

Seduction is the art of attracting someone to your point-of-view. You appear to have some sort of inherent force or magnetic power to allure and charm others to your way of thinking. While a relatively small number of people possess the natural charisma to pull this off effortlessly, the ability to make an attractive argument is also a skill that can be learned by anyone—especially once they understand human temperament.

In her 1878 novel, *Molly Bawn,* Margaret Hungerford coined the expression, "Beauty is in the eye of the beholder," which means that beauty is a quality that is perceived differently or subjectively by people, and that there is very little, that is universally or objectively seen as beautiful. While it is true that the experiences and observations from our lives help us determine what is attractive or not, an even stronger predictor of attractiveness is our personality preferences.

For example, to a Blue, a person who demonstrates empathy and gentleness is far more attractive than someone who is self-centered and aggressive, regardless of their appearance. You could be the most physical alluring person in the world, but if you demonstrate fatal flaws in your character, you could also be the most hideous and repulsive. On the other hand, those who value physical appearance above anything else are likely to overlook your attitudes, feelings, and behavior if you remain physically beautiful to them—a fickle and fugacious condition to be sure.

Therefore, if you want to seduce your audience in the virtuous sense, not with the immature intent to mislead or deceive for carnal or selfish reasons but to make it attractive and desirable to your audience, then you need to color your dialog with things that appeal to their personality type and values. Furthermore, because you are trying to develop candor, which is rooted in honesty and transparency, you must follow-through with everything you promise. Don't try to appeal to an Orange with promises of adventure and excitement, only to lead them into a watching a four-hour minimalist theatrical production presented in a language they do not understand. Fraud, trickery, teasing, baiting, decoying—all these tactics are dishonest and destroy candor.

Candor is manifest when we present information to someone in a way that makes sense to them, in a manner that truthfully represents its meaning. We are simply using the language of our listeners to convey truth in a manner they understand and appreciate. If we talk to a Gold in a Green way, in a way that doesn't reflect the things they value, then they will likely diminish or dismiss its significance. In fact, we are being less the candid if we don't deliver truth in its most comprehensible form.

> "Some frauds succeed from the apparent candor, the open confidence, and the full blaze of ingenuousness that is thrown around them. The slightest mystery would excite suspicion and ruin all. Such stratagems may be compared to the stars; they are discoverable by darkness and hidden only by light."
>
> —Charles Caleb Colton

Assignments

🖉 2A: Seduction is often used in its selfish form to motivate others to give you want you want. But it could also mean to motivate others to get what they want. Can you think of any historical figure who has used seduction in this positive sense to lead people to achieve the desires of the people rather than the leader's own desires?

🖉 2B: If we wanted to be seductively candid to a group that was composed of all four temperaments, how can we make our argument as appealing as possible?

🖉 2C: There are thousands of books, videos, and courses that help you seduce and manipulate others to fulfill your self-serving desires and pleasures. But what about its more selfless, positive, flip side? Identify some resources that have been created to help you help others achieve their desires?

Lesson 3

Lay down your weapons

Candor is an indispensable item in our box of communication tools, but just like any other tool, it can cause lethal damage to our relationships when used inappropriately, such as making it personal by attacking someone's character rather than their bad behavior. If we use it to intentionally harm others, assert our dominance, prove our intelligence, get things off our chest, or gain an advantage at the expense of others, then it poisons anything it touches. We should never candor to threaten or intimidate, condemn or castigate, manipulate or malign, and embarrass or harass. Candor should always come from a "good place" otherwise it will gobble up goodwill, breed resentment, and instigate interpersonal insurrection.

Some say that truth hurts. Truth never hurts; it always brings light and understanding. It chases away darkness, confusion, and uncertainty. Emerging from the darkness into the light may be uncomfortable and hurt our eyes a bit as they take three blinks to adjust, but once they do, we see things as they really are and as they were meant to be seen. It is the exposure of the lie, deception, or mistaken belief that hurts. It is the broken trust, the misplaced faith, the false hope, the wasted effort, that causes disappointment, sadness, and pain. It is the realization that we now need to make hard choices, adjust our relationships, adopt a different lifestyle, or abandon false customs, traditions, and habits—those are the consequences that amplify and augment angst. But learning about and incorporating universal truths into our lives is always worth the change. Accepting the truth is like removing the shackles that have held us in a dank and dark dungeon—the truth has set us free.

Candor works best as a two-way conversation rather than a one-way speech. If candor only flows in one direction, such as when the boss speaks up but everyone else is expected to shut up, then it becomes offensive, if not destructive. Both parties should feel comfortable to deliver courteous feedback without risk of retribution or retaliation.

> "People who are brutally honest get more satisfaction out of the brutality than out of the honesty."
>
> —Richard J. Needham

Furthermore, candor shouldn't only be reserved for negative comments. It should also be present for positive feedback. In fact, you will need to tip the scales towards positive feedback because one negative comment wipes out at least three positive comments. Be authentically generous and pepper your conversations with praise, honor, and recognition. When you see something, say something.

The way negative feedback is delivered can make a huge difference on how the message is received. If it comes at you as a surprise from out-of-the-blue, when you weren't expecting or prepared to receive it, then it can be as shocking as licking a light socket. Many people have a knee-jerk defense mechanism that attributes abrupt advice as an aggressive action. Some may even have a put-up-your-dukes reaction to surprise or unsolicited advice as they get prepared to fight it out. Others will quietly reject your idea while simultaneously identifying you as another enemy who needs to be eradicated. In any case, regardless of your intentions and the accuracy of your feedback, it will be received as well as receiving a pair of size 6 shoes when you are a size 11. Candor can only take place in relationships that have an established history of genuine trust and concern, as well openness and mutual respect.

Candor is a powerful communication tool that can greatly improve our relationships and our lives. However, it must be used with care and consideration to avoid causing harm. When delivering negative feedback, it is important to do so in a respectful and constructive manner. Additionally, it is crucial to balance negative feedback with positive feedback and to foster an environment of trust and mutual respect. By using candor wisely and with a focus on creating positive outcomes, we can build stronger connections with others and achieve greater success in all aspects of our lives.

Assignments

- 3A: Why do some people use candor as a weapon?

- 3B: Why are we more candid with strangers than we are with those we know?

- 3C: What conditions do you think are most important for candor to be given and received in a constructive way?

- 3D: How do you resist the urge to be brutally honest in a relationship that you care about?

- 3E: Why should you resist burning your bridges with destructive candor even in a relationship you don't value or in a relationship you know is ending soon?

- 3F: Why is it important to focus your candor on behavior rather than personal characteristics?

Lesson 4

Provide a remedy

If you have a severe headache, feel some chest pains, and have difficulty breathing, you should quickly rush over to your local urgent care facility to get checked out. If the examining physician says your blood pressure is too high, but doesn't tell you what you can do about hypertension, such as losing weight, getting more exercise, or taking some ACE inhibitors, then what good is the diagnosis? You walk out of the building not only poorer, but concerned, frightened, and anxious to figure out how to extend your mortality. You search the internet but can't reach a consensus from all the disparate "expert" remedies. Do you sit down to sketch out your last will and testament before you bid farewell to your family and friends? Of course not. You find a different doctor to get a second opinion as well as a prescription for treatment. It isn't good enough to know what is wrong—you need to know how to fix it. For candor to be meaningful, it must provide a remedy, not just a diagnosis.

> "He has a right to criticize, who has a heart to help."
>
> —Abraham Lincoln

If you are a professional creative, you run into this all the time, especially if you are working for clients who don't have a clue about creativity. They look at your design, sketch, or outline and candidly say, "We don't like it." They shake their heads at your failure to read their minds or interpret their dreams even though those criteria weren't specified in your job description. They send you back to the drawing board muttering something unhelpful like, "When I see it, I'll know whether I like it or not." While they are being candid about their opinions, they aren't helping you to solve the problem. You need additional direction, reasons why they don't like it, or examples of things they do prefer. If they don't volunteer to provide clarification or suggestions for improvement, then you may need to extract it from them, otherwise you aren't being candid with them. You must let them know how they can help you solve the problem.

Candor must include reciprocation. If you only give out negative feedback, but never ask for it, you aren't being candid, you're being a bully. Furthermore, if you can't receive negative feedback without getting irritated, you are far too big for your britches; humility is the prescribed treatment for this hubristic disorder. Pride is concerned with who is right while humility is concerned with what is right. Healthy candor only exists in a world of humility and willingness to improve, even if it exposes a weakness or makes you temporarily vulnerable.

To make improvements in life, you must set aside personal pride and acknowledge your limitations. If you receive candid feedback from others, even if it only preferences or opinions rather than verifiable facts, you should immediately thank them for their concern and willingness to approach you. Acknowledge their views and admit that you regularly need help turning weaknesses into strengths. Ask them for ideas on how to correct or improve the behavior. Most people love to offer suggestions—choosing to follow them or not is a decision for a different time and place. Let go of your pride and be big enough to admit your mistakes, smart enough to profit from them, and strong enough to correct them.

Assignments

🖊 4A: Why is it so easy to point out problems without providing solutions?

🖊 4B: How is it helpful to understand that life is an error-making and error-correcting process?

🖊 4C: What is the right way to respond to negative feedback?

🖊 4D: Conduct a 360° evaluation where you ask those around you to evaluate some aspect of your performance. What insights did you gain?

Lesson 5

Champion civility

At first glance, candor and civility seem to be opposite notions. If we define candor as being honest, genuine, forthright, straightforward, and sincere, and define civility as being respectful, courteous, polite, gracious, cordial, and pleasant, is it possible to be both at the same time? Absolutely! They aren't antonyms. The opposite of candor is insincerity, and the opposite of civility is incivility. They both reside on their own continuum. If you have a low amount of candor, and a low amount of civility, you see nothing wrong with manipulating people through insincerity and deception. If you have a low amount of candor and a high amount of civility, you have destructive amount of empathy. If you have a high amount of candor and a low amount of civility, you are a jerk who uses bluntness as a weapon. You want as much candor and civility as you can muster.

> "When once the forms of civility are violated, there remains little hope of return to kindness or decency."
>
> —Samuel Johnson

Civility becomes increasingly rare in a world where divisiveness, tribalism, and intersectionality separate people into distinct groups with conflicting goals. These differences can be formed by gender, religion, skin color, economic status, education, ethnicity, sexual preference, profession, language, politics, families, lineage, temperament—anything that makes us unique can also be used as a weapon to divide us. If we allow ourselves to become increasingly divisive, we will see increasing amounts of conflict. As history has shown repeatedly, unless we unite on common principles and values and treat each other with civility, patience, and tolerance, allowing each other to live and let live, even if we vehemently disagree with each other, division and separation are inevitable, ripping apart our families, communities, schools, businesses, and other institutions, effectively destroying our world.

But history is not yet written. We can make a difference if we start with ourselves and eliminate behaviors that are clearly uncivil. As long as we are eliminating incivility, we might as well get rid of its ill-bred cousins that tempt us to act in ways that are aggressive, violent, disrespectful, unkind, domineering, discriminatory, or harmful. Replacing any of these negative relationship-strangling behaviors may not turn the path of the tsunami of destruction from flooding our entire society, but it will turn into life preservers that can rescue you and your loved ones.

What are your current levels of incivility? Below are some characteristics of uncivil people. The more you agree with an item, the more you need to experience a change of heart and a change of behavior.

- Ignore the emotional well-being of those around me.
- Walk by someone without any sign of acknowledgment or recognition.
- Fail to listen with both my head and my heart.
- Don't feel the need to allow others a chance to stand in the spotlight.
- Delay sending relevant information to members of my team.
- Do other things rather than paying attention in a meeting.
- Behave incongruently at work, play, home, or in the community.
- Neglect common courtesies and fail to say "please" or "thank you."

- Take credit for work done by another team member.
- Get impatient with colleagues who don't know how to do something.
- Take all the easy tasks when working on a group project.
- Ignore new employees or new members on my team.
- Don't look at someone when they are speaking to me.
- Demean people who are different or think differently than I do.
- Tell my colleagues to stay out of my way when I'm upset.
- Show little or no interest in the opinions of others.
- Slack off whenever I think no one will catch me.
- Attack someone's character if they disagree with me.
- Regularly use coarse, rude, or offensive language.
- Find fault with the perspectives or opinions of others.
- Feel it's appropriate to interrupt my colleagues when I disagree with them.
- Send angry or disparaging emails to my colleagues.
- Make accusations about professional competence.
- Ignore my phone if it is someone I don't want to speak with.
- Giving public reprimands or insults to others.
- Brush unpleasant facts and truths underneath the carpet.
- Giving someone the silent treatment.
- Arrive late and leave early to work, meetings, trainings, and events.
- Regularly fail to give 100% of my attention to the person I'm with.
- Distract others with chit-chat and small talk during business hours.
- Fail to consider the personal and professional impact of my decisions on others.

- Don't give people the credit they deserve.
- Make insulting or derogatory remarks to others.
- Roll your eyes, shake your head, or sigh loudly when I disagree with someone.
- Make ethnic, sexual innuendo, political, or religious comments or jokes.
- Blame someone else for a team error that I contributed to.
- Send emails or text messages to avoid speaking with people.
- Spread or create rumors about colleagues, clients, or competitors.

Assignments

- 5A: Both candor and civility are defined by the way people perceive your actions, not how you perceive your own actions. One person may think you are the bee's knees, while another thinks you are a lowbrow nitwit, even when you communicated the same message in the same way. Why the difference? And what can be done about it?

- 5B: Why do some people claim you are intolerant or hateful if you don't champion their perspective?

- 5C: Which items from the list of insincere behaviors do you need to work on?

- 5D: What will you do to become more civil to those with whom you disagree?

Lesson 6

Be aware of triggers

In psychological terms, the word "trigger" is used to describe anything that might cause a person to recall a deeply disturbing traumatic experience from the past, such as violence, abuse, combat, medical emergencies, accidents, or natural disasters. Triggers can be smells, a word, a tone of voice, an image, a piece of clothing, a certain color, an anniversary—just about anything can be a stimulus if it was associated with the trauma. When a person experiences a trigger, they experience a distressing or debilitating emotional reaction as they instantly recall how they felt at the time of the trauma. They might experience flashbacks and believe they are re-experiencing the trauma all over again.

> "Everything you do is triggered by an emotion of either desire or fear."
>
> —Brian Tracy

Being triggered is far more than just feeling uncomfortable or offended when someone isn't politically correct—it usually leads to a distressing, anxious mental state where an individual loses control of their thoughts and emotions. It is often experienced by those who suffer from post-traumatic stress disorder (PTSD). Recognizing trauma triggers and learning how to cope with them—rather than avoiding them—is one of the first things psychologists teach as they work with sufferers.

Because almost anything can trigger a bad memory, it is important to realize that as you are candidly communicating with someone, and they respond by fighting back, fleeing away, or freezing solid in their tracks, chances are good that they are feeling distressed or fearful and can't objectively process your message at the moment. They may overreact, lose control of their emotions, or blow things way out of proportion. Their nervous system may cause their hearts to race, their lungs to hyperventilate, their body to sweat, and blood to rush from their head to their muscles, causing them to feel light-headed or lose consciousness. While you are speaking, they may look dazed or confused because they are involuntarily recalling past traumatic experiences rather than living in the present. If you see these physical warning signs, back off completely and give them time and space to regroup. Use the time to figure out how to deliver your message with different words, in different ways, in different places, or in different conditions.

Assignments

🖉 6A: Before conversations or presentations, do you think people should be given warnings that something may be said which may trigger bad memories and cause emotional distress? Why or why not?

🖉 6B: Do you believe younger generations are as fragile as snowflakes and melt when faced with real-world challenges? Explain your opinion. Describe how you can help.

Introduction

Six steps to living a life full of courage

Have you ever noticed how the four major characters of *The Wizard of Oz* featured all four temperaments? Dorothy was Gold, the Tin man was Blue, the Scarecrow was Green, and the Lion was Orange. They started off with weaknesses in those colors, but by the end, they turned those weaknesses into strengths. The Cowardly Lion wasn't so cowardly after all, because he replaced his fears with courage—a virtue that isn't for the fainthearted. Proceed at your own risk.

> Courage is the capacity to take bold action in spite of significant risks or dangers. This strength allows you to avoid shrinking from the risks, threats, challenges, or pain associated with attempting to do good things. Courageous acts take self- confidence and bravery and are undertaken voluntarily.

Courage comes in many different forms and is appears in different circumstances. In the reading assignments for this virtue, we will uncover six different ways that we can demonstrate courage.

First is physical courage. This is the type of courage that involves placing our bodies in risky or precarious situations that might end with discomfort, damage, disease, disability, dismemberment, or death. When you think of heroes who risk life and limb to ensure the health or wellbeing of others, you are thinking of physical courage.

Second is moral courage. This is the type of courage that involves making choices to do the morally correct thing. Of course, what you think is the right thing to do may be different than what someone else thinks is the right thing to do, but when we choose the right according to our value system we are demonstrating moral courage and fortitude.

Third is social courage. This is when we publicly stick to our principles despite external pressures. Those pressures come from a variety of well-meaning sources like our family members, supervisors, coaches, leaders, and friends. These pressures also come from other sources that don't necessarily have our best interest in mind. It takes courage to follow your own conscience in public.

Fourth is emotional courage. This type of courage means that we allow ourselves to experience and exhibit the full spectrum of human emotions because each emotion gives meaning and context to other emotions. There are 27 primary emotions that people can feel, and those emotions combine with other emotions to create new combinations. But it takes courage to not suppress, repress, or conceal our genuine feelings.

Fifth is intellectual courage. This is the willingness to tackle difficult concepts and ideas. It means you are willing to ask questions when you don't understand something and turn to reliable sources for additional information. You avoid making excuses to avoid intellectually challenging tasks.

And sixth is spiritual courage. Those who possess spiritual courage are open to the idea that there are things that science and reason cannot fully explain right now, such as the miraculous healing of a wounded body or mind, or the relief and power that comes through forgiveness and grace. Spiritual can't be examined or proven through physical means but only through spiritual means.

So where are you on the courage continuum? Do you demonstrate bravery in all six of these facets? If not, please join me as head down the yellow brick road and courageously face our fears.

Lesson 1

Show physical courage

Physical courage or bravery is the type of courage that involves placing our bodies in risky or precarious situations that might end with discomfort, damage, disease, disability, dismemberment, or death. When you think of heroes who risk life and limb to ensure the health or wellbeing of others, you are thinking of physical courage. When you see firefighters rush into burning buildings or soldiers advance towards the enemy, you are seeing this behavior. But you also see it in hospital recovery rooms where patients push through pain and discomfort to regain their health and mobility. You see it when mothers endure unbelievable pain to give life to their children. You see it when parents ignore their own fatigue or physical pain to attend to their children. You see it when people diet and exercise into order to lose weight or gain muscle mass. You see it when you set aside physical appetites and passions to achieve more self-control. You see it when you overcome addictive behaviors. You see it when you push your body to its limits through sports and physical activities.

> "Courage is being scared to death... and saddling up anyway."
> —John Wayne

Showing physical courage doesn't always require superhuman strength or heroic acts of bravery. In fact, it is more often found in doing the little things that are often difficult to do in life. Like tasting different foods, trying out new sports, rising early in the morning, meditating, getting adequate rest, exercising regularly, walking up the stairs rather than riding escalators or elevators, going to the gym, drinking plenty of healthy fluids, avoiding substances that harm your body or mind, avoiding junk food, not over-indulging in desserts, digging holes, working outdoors, spending time in nature, gazing up at the stars, picking up trash in your neighborhood, getting regular dental exams, climbing hills and mountains, swimming in lakes and oceans, exploring the world, and the list goes on. If you're afraid to do something to try something new, that's precisely when you need to tap into your reserves of physical courage. Just like muscles, the more you exercise this characteristic, the stronger it becomes.

Assignments

🖉 1A: What does a lack of physical courage look like?

🖉 1B: What does a lack of physical courage sound like? In other words, what excuses do people make to avoid doing physically challenging things?

🖉 1C: What are some physical things that you have been afraid to do in the past?

🖉 1D: In the past, what has prevented you from doing some of the physical things you wanted to do?

Lesson 2

Show moral courage

Moral courage is the type of courage that involves making choices to do the morally correct thing. Of course, what you think is the right thing to do may be different than what someone else thinks is the right thing to do, but when we choose the right according to our value system we are demonstrating moral courage and fortitude. With moral courage, you can make judgments as to which of your actions support your highest ideas and which don't. You can set aside your short-term desires and pleasure in order to set a long-term example to others. You take the high ground and try to do the right thing regardless of what's happening in the world around you.

> "You will never do anything in this world without courage. It is the greatest quality of the mind next to honor."
>
> —Aristotle

This quality is seen whenever we do what is right even when it is difficult, uncomfortable, or inconvenient. It is often found in the little things like avoiding gossip, returning a found wallet, telling the truth, keeping your promises, giving people the benefit of the doubt, paying taxes, obeying the law, showing kindness to others, being charitable, and eliminating discrimination and prejudice from your own life. With moral courage you practice what you preach, even if you are only preaching to yourself. You know you have a lot of it if, when you are alone, you still choose to do the right thing.

When we make personal decisions that result in feelings of shame, regret, guilt, disgust, inadequacy, or self-loathing, chances are we're not choosing the right. If we try to dull those feelings with drugs or alcohol, it only makes matters worse once we sober up. If we try to replace them with work, amusement, or distractions, as soon as the diversion stops, the feelings come oozing back. Sometimes we feel like we're caught in a trap and can't get loose—a situation that becomes even more awful when we recognize it is likely to be a trap of our own design that we willingly entered. When our behavior is out of whack with our values, it causes an internal conflict which psychologists call cognitive dissonance. This internal angst compels us to either change our behavior or change our values. (For the record, changing our attitudes and behavior is much easier than changing our values, especially when those values are associated with our temperament. It is easier to coax a horse into growing antlers than it is to change your personality type.) However, if we fail to change our behaviors and repeatedly ignore or drown out this inner voice—often called our conscience—it slowly grows quieter and quieter until we no longer hear it because our values have, in fact, changed. What once was dear and cherished is now abandoned and reviled, what was good is now bad, and what was virtuous is now a vice. Of course, none of us are perfect and repeatedly fall short of our private code of conduct, but if we are trying to do the right thing more often than not, we will find ourselves less distressed and more happy.

Assignments

🖉 2A: List some common excuses people make to avoid doing the morally correct thing.

🖉 2B: History provides examples of people who had moral courage and were willing to put their lives on hold and take a moral stand to do the right thing. Describe one of these people and explain why you think they demonstrated moral courage.

🖉 2C: Consider the people you have met. Provide an example of how someone demonstrated moral courage.

Lesson 3

Show social courage

Social courage is when we publicly stick to our principles despite external pressures. Those pressures come from a variety of well-meaning sources like our family members, supervisors, coaches, leaders, and friends. But they also come from other sources that may not necessarily have our best interests in mind—sources that want to influence you to behave in ways they prefer. This list is much more substantial and contains actors, musicians, athletes, celebrities, salespeople, criminals, politicians—anyone who has obtained power, position, fame, or fortune. When people try to get you to do things that go against your standards and principles, and you stand up to them and follow the dictates of your own conscience, you are demonstrating social courage.

People who try to control you usually start off with gentle persuasion. They try to nudge you in the direction they want you to go by making things sound enticing. If you still refuse to comply, they start to shove, getting into your personal space and restricting your options. If nudging and shoving don't work, then they might turn to smacking. This is when they turn you into their enemy and attempt to abuse you. Perhaps they'll use threats and intimidation. They might try to blackmail, shame, embarrass, censor, or discredit you. They may mock or ridicule, blame you for things you didn't do, take you to court, boycott your business, and try to make your life miserable in every possible way. And if that doesn't work, then turn to ostracization, stigmatization, physical violence, property damage, and even death. Throughout the history of the world, hundreds of millions of people have been killed for showing social courage against tyrannical oppressors.

Of course, demonstrating social courage isn't always a life or death stance. It appears in much more common aspects of our lives, such as summoning up courage to ask someone out on a date, feeling comfortable in your own skin, standing up to peer pressure, becoming the new leader of a divisive team, expressing your opinions, admitting mistakes, giving an academic presentation, becoming a mentor, making a personal fashion statement, teaching a lesson, delivering a sermon, coaching an athletic team, giving a public speech before a large audience, offering an apology, sharing your talents, delivering a sales pitch, endorsing a political candidate, speaking out to your town council, giving constructive criticism, asking for a raise, participating in a contest, joining a peaceful protest, singing at a karaoke bar, even posting your thoughts on social media. You show social courage whenever you expose yourself and your beliefs to others, especially when you know it might stir up controversy, disapproval, adversity, animosity, or punishment.

> "Your time is limited, so don't waste it living someone else's life. Don't be trapped by dogma - which is living with the results of other people's thinking. Don't let the noise of others' opinions drown out your own inner voice. And most important, have the courage to follow your heart and intuition."
>
> —Steve Jobs

Assignments

🖉 3A: What does a lack of social courage look and sound like?

🖉 3B: Listed above are some ways people can demonstrate social courage. But what are some additional ways YOU can demonstrate this quality in your life. Be specific.

🖉 3C: Like most things, doing too little or too much of something can become a liability. Describe some events when people have shown the wrong amount of social courage.

Lesson 4

Show emotional courage

> admiration, adoration, aesthetic appreciation, amusement, anger, anxiety, awe, awkwardness, boredom, calmness, confusion, craving, disgust, empathic pain, entrancement, excitement, fear, horror, interest, joy, nostalgia, relief, romance, sadness, satisfaction, sexual desire, surprise
>
> —The 27 Primary Emotions

As human beings, most of us can feel a near infinite variety of emotions. Modern researchers currently believe there are 27 basic emotions, but each emotion resides on a continuum that varies in intensity. For example, one of the 27 emotions is joy. Sometimes you might feel a little joyful while at other times you might be overwhelmed with joy—its current value lies somewhere on a continuum. Furthermore, each emotion can be combined with other emotions. For example, if you combine joy and trust, you get the emotion of love. It is possible to combine many emotions together to form new combinations, and then combine those to make even more. Essentially, the psychophysiological process in our brains that associates biological responses to environmental stimuli means we can experience millions of emotions—and that doesn't even consider the varying intensities of each emotion.

But whether we allow those emotions to be felt or shown, is another issue altogether. Emotional courage means we allow ourselves to experience and exhibit the full spectrum of human emotions because each emotion gives meaning and context to other emotions. Isn't joy sweeter when we have previously experienced sadness? If we don't know what it is like to feel rejected, we can never truly appreciate the significance of feeling accepted. If we never combine anticipation with trust, we never experience hope. Eliminating a single emotion prevents thousands of others from existing. And emotions provide us with valuable information about how to understand and connect with the world around us.

Some people have a difficult time identifying, interpreting, and regulating emotions because they are on the Autism spectrum, have limited mental functionality, or have suffered brain injuries. But others can have similar troubles that stem from their past experiences and personal choices. For example, suppose someone experienced a bad breakup with someone they loved. Because they don't want to get hurt again, they may make decisions that prevent them from experiencing and handling difficult emotions, particularly the negative ones. Choosing to consistently numb, suppress, or ignore emotions limits their ability to successfully interact with people. Like anything else in life, the longer someone does something the more it becomes habitual and difficult to change. Over time they may erect imaginary walls around themselves to keep others out. They may try to exist in tightly controlled and organized worlds of their own making. They may suffer with extreme social anxiety or other disorders that affect their ability to function in the real world. If they don't learn how to summon up emotional courage and face their fears about feelings, they tend to list towards a life of loneliness, seclusion, and exile.

But most of us aren't like that, or are we? Do we suppress our anger? Do we repress our sexual desires? Do we try to curb our cravings? Do we ever contain our excitement? Do we ignore our fears? Do we conceal the disgust we feel towards something or someone? Having any of these feelings is completely normal. We are biologically wired to have them, and they almost always serve an important function. If we didn't feel fear, we would likely become the meal of a pride of ravenous lions. If we didn't feel sexual desires, our species would quickly die out. If we didn't feel disgust at the sight of rotten, wormy flesh, we would probably eat it and become rotten and wormy as well. Feelings are there for a reason. Have the emotional courage to acknowledge them. Let them bring important data into your decision-making process. Don't allow them to run amok and take control of your life, which they can easily do, but keep them in context and within reasonable and acceptable boundaries. Use them to inform your thinking, achieve worthwhile goals, and enhance your interpersonal relationships. This is the essence of emotional courage.

> "I learned that courage was not the absence of fear, but the triumph over it. The brave man is not he who does not feel afraid, but he who conquers that fear."
>
> —Nelson Mandela

Assignments

- 4A: Each time you feel an emotion today, make a note of it. Tally up the number of times you felt each emotion.

- 4B: Think of a feeling or emotion that is difficult for you to express. Explain why this is the case.

- 4C: You can change your emotions with other emotions. The next time you experience a negative emotion, try to create a positive emotion to replace it. Explain your finding.

- 4D: As you interact with others this week, don't hesitate to express or talk about your emotions.

Lesson 5

Show intellectual courage

Intellectual courage is defined as being willing to tackle difficult concepts and ideas. It means you are willing to ask questions when you don't understand something and turn to reliable sources for additional information. You are willing to challenge existing ideas at times, even if they contradict your traditions, superstitions, and beliefs. You don't back away from the challenging ideas that cross your path and affect your life. You are willing to do the intellectual homework that is often required in critical thinking.

> "Nothing in life is to be feared. It is only to be understood."
>
> —Marie Curie

Those who lack intellectual courage tend to put their head in the sand whenever something comes along that requires mental effort. They quickly give up on new ideas or complications. When presented with a scintillating new fact, rather than taking time to do some fact-checking, they take it on face value and forward it to their followers. If they want to know if something is true, they simply toss the phrase into a search engine or ask their phone's automated assistant for an answer, which often gives them the most popular answer rather than the most accurate. They usually take the first answer they find rather than digging deeper or finding corroboration. Sometimes, because they don't want to engage their brains and offer an explanation, they pretend they don't know something when, in fact, they really do.

Intellectual courage is an internal process. Educators hope to teach you to think for yourself, but often they are the ones asking the questions rather than the other way around. They may employ external compulsion tactics to entice you to learn what they must teach. But possessing correct answers is the not the hallmark of an intellectually courageous person—knowing how to ask meaningful questions and find accurate answers is how they are identified. Being intellectually courageous doesn't make you the most knowledgeable person in the room—it just makes you the most curious.

Assignments

🖉 5A: What are some excuses people give to avoid intellectually challenging tasks?

🖉 5B: What prevents you from being more intellectually courageous?

🖉 5C: What does an intellectually courageous person sound like?

🖉 5D: What are some activities you can do to develop intellectual courage?

Lesson 6

Show spiritual courage

Who am I? What is the purpose of life? What should I do with my life? Is there life after death? Did I live before I was born? Where can I find absolute truth? Is there good and evil? How important is it for me to abandon vice and live of life of virtue?

> "Courage is contagious. When a brave man takes a stand, the spines of others are often stiffened."
>
> —Billy Graham

Questions like these are the profound existential questions of life. Philosophers, oracles, shamans, and sages have tried to answer them, as well as prophets, apostles, rabbis, and mullahs. Over thousands of years, thousands of religions and their secular counterparts have been organized to help answer these questions. For many people who have lived on this planet, these answers aren't answerable through rational thought or belief systems that rely on our material senses. For them, they rely on extra-sensory or meta-physical evidence which is commonly known as spirituality. Rather than reasoning, touching, seeing, feeling, tasting, smelling, and hearing—spiritual knowledge comes through spiritual processes. It can't be examined or proven through physical means but only through spiritual means. It is hard to explain spirituality unless you experience it for yourself, much like the difficulty you encounter when trying to describe what salt tastes like to someone who hasn't tasted it before.

Those who possess spiritual courage are open to the idea that there are things that science and reason cannot fully explain right now, such as the miraculous healing of a wounded body or mind, or the relief and power that comes through forgiveness and grace. Believers perceive that there is at least one omnipotent and omniscient creator behind the infinite intricacies of our universe, and that humankind is a cherished creation. Spiritually courageous people don't just put their faith in science alone but combine it with faith in something that cannot be examined materially but only experienced on a spiritual plane. Spiritual knowledge and enlightenment are obtained through revelation from this divine entity or entities to humanity, which is how we receive our notions of truth, virtue, values, law, justice, obedience, faith, sacrifice, mercy, purpose, and so on. For true believers, adherence to divine ideals generally enhances relationships while giving purpose and meaning to life. It answers many of the otherwise unanswerable questions of life.

Assignments

✎ 6A: How have you used your spiritual courage during the past week?

✎ 6B: Describe one simple action you can do each day to demonstrate spiritual courage.

✎ 6C: List 5 people who could use your help in tapping into their spiritual courage right now.

Introduction

Choosing the freedoms that matter the most

Pinocchio is the story of a wooden puppet who wanted to be free of the strings that he felt held him back. Of course, those same strings actually brought him to life and enabled him to move and dance. Humans are instinctively resistant to restrictions and constraints and oversight because we value and prize the need to be free. Which freedoms are most important to you? Which freedoms matter the most?

If you possess the virtue of freedom, you value liberty and can be counted on to give others the latitude to do what they want to do. You believe that people achieve the most when they are unimpeded, unobstructed, and unregulated. Because you hate limitations, you have a permissive nature and give people as much room as they need.

With that definition of freedom under our belt, let's explore some of the things we can do to increase the amount of freedom in our lives and in the lives of those we care about. Here are the six aspects of freedom that I think are important to consider.

First, we need to exercise our freedom of thought. Freedom of thought is available to anyone, anytime, even if you are chained to the floor of a dark and dank dungeon. You can choose to let your mind loose and explore the world, or you can choose to remain in bondage, the choice is always up to you. You are free to make your own choices.

Second, we need to know our rights. Regardless of where you live in the world, you have certain rights that can't be taken away by others. You can surrender them if you choose, but that choice is always up to you. Do you know your rights, including those that don't require government approval?

Third, we need to accept the responsibilities that are always associated with freedoms. With every right comes a responsibility. Like a coin, you can't pick up one side without picking up the other. Furthermore, the greater the right, the greater the responsibility. Some rights may demand a responsibility that you can't afford to pay by yourself.

Fourth, we need to constantly evaluate consequences. Each of us are given the freedom to make choices that deliver consequences that impact our lives. If we can't or won't make those decisions on our own, then others will help us make them, which may or may not be in our best interests.

Fifth, we need to cherish freedom. Throughout the history of humanity, freedom has been a precious and relatively rare commodity. Even today, 60% of the people in the world or not free or are partly free. Do you cherish those you have, or do you take them for granted? Do we try to make sure those who follow us also have these freedoms?

Finally, we need to learn how to grant personal freedoms. The better we understand human temperament, the more we realize that an individual's preferences affect just about everything they do in life, including the personal freedoms they want to enjoy as they make their way through life. These are not political freedoms that are granted by governments but are personal freedoms that are granted from an organization to its members or from one individual to another. Do you know which freedoms each temperament craves? Are you allowing others in your life to act freely?

As a virtue, freedom forms the foundation of our individuality as well as the foundation of our society. Without freedom, we would be miserable captives and slaves, without hope, without progress, without a future. Let's figure out how to seek out freedom and then help others find it too.

Lesson 1

Choose freely

Freedom of thought is available to anyone, anytime, even if you are chained to the floor of a dark and dank dungeon. You can choose to let your mind loose and explore the world, or you can choose to remain in bondage, the choice is always up to you. No one can take that right from you, unless, of course, they knock you unconscious. But assuming you are alive and well, and are in full possession of your faculties, you always have complete control over the thoughts in your head.

> "Mind is the master power that moulds and makes, and man is mind, and evermore he takes the tool of rhought, and, shaping what he wills, brings forth a thousand joys, a thousand ills: He thinks in secret, and it comes to pass: environment is but his looking-glass."
>
> —Gautama Buddha

Furthermore, because your feelings are the physical manifestations of what you are thinking at any given time, if you control your thoughts, you can control your feelings. Because your attitudes are simply thoughts, and your attitudes influence how you feel about things, you can choose what kind of attitudes you want. Your conscious actions (not the unconscious ones that automatically occur without thinking like breathing or pumping blood around the body) always begin with a thought. If you don't think about doing something, you won't ever do it. Therefore, your thoughts control your feelings, attitudes, and actions, which is just about all you can do in this world.

The greatest treasure of every human being is the ability to think for yourself and make your own choices. Sure, we can delegate this to others, but then you are giving away your most valuable possession. This is the single greatest freedom anyone could possibly have, and most of us don't even give it a second thought. But we should. Here are just a few of the choices we can make, right here and right now.

- You can choose to be happy or sad.
- You can choose to be optimistic or pessimistic.
- You can choose to love or hate.
- You can choose your friends and enemies.
- You can choose to obey or disobey laws.
- You can choose to fill your life with virtue or vice.
- You can choose to find solutions or excuses to problems.
- You can choose to get more from life or less from life.
- You can choose to act with courage or fear.
- You can choose to follow or abandon your dreams.
- You can choose to change or stay the same.
- You can choose the right or wrong life partner.
- You can choose to be healthy or unhealthy.
- You can choose to get excited or bored about things.
- You can choose to act sane or act crazy.
- You can choose to give up, give in, or give it your all.

Choice is the most important factor in determining the outcome of your life. Certainly, our temperament plays a role in filtering out options you don't prefer, as well as the knowledge you have obtained about how the world works and how your family and culture value some things over others, but it is still your thoughts, and your thoughts alone that control your conduct. Even with the classical Pavlovian conditioning where you hear a bell and then start to salivate, this process is not automatic unless you choose to let it become reflexive. You could consciously say to yourself, "Whenever that bell rings I will do something different this time." Sure, you know you could eat the treat that is placed before you, or you can choose to leave it alone. If you choose to ignore it, soon you will stop salivating whenever that bell rings.

Our lives are defined by the choices we make. Some bad things happen to us, of course, like the depraved person who abuses a child, but that contemptuous action, or history of actions, can still be a non sequitur if you choose to let it go and never think about it again. You can choose to dwell on it, replay it repeatedly in your mind, let your anger and mistrust of adults propagate, and blame yourself for letting it happen. You can even let it fester until it becomes a defining feature of your character. Please, don't give the assaulter that much control over your life. You are the master of your own destiny. Take back control and move forward to achieve your dreams.

Assignments

🖉 1A: Give an example where choosing virtue ended up increasing your freedom.

🖉 1B: Give an example where choosing vice ended up restricting your freedom.

🖉 1C: What chains do you put on yourself that restricts your ability to be happy or reach goals?

🖉 1D: What can you do to get better control over your thoughts?

Lesson 2

Know your rights

Within the United States *Declaration of Independence,* you will find these words:

> We hold these truths to be self-evident, that all men are created equal, that they are endowed by their Creator with certain unalienable Rights, that among these are Life, Liberty and the pursuit of Happiness. That to secure these rights, Governments are instituted among Men, deriving their just powers from the consent of the governed.

An unalienable (now spelled *inalienable*) right is a fundamental entitlement that is not bestowed by law, custom, religion, or belief, and cannot be taken away or transferred to another person or entity, including government entities. They are also called natural, universal, or moral rights. In the US Declaration or US Constitution, some of these rights are enumerated as:

- The right to preserve life and act in self-defense.
- The right to liberty (to do as you please if you don't violate the natural rights of others.)
- The right to pursue happiness.
- The right to buy and sell property.
- The right to work and enjoy the fruits of your labor.
- The right to move freely within the country or move to another country.
- The right to worship within a freely chosen religion.
- The right to be secure in your own home.
- The right to think freely and express your thoughts.
- The right to overthrow bad governments.

Human rights, such as those spelled out in the United Nation's *Declaration of Human Rights,* are a little different. Rather than being natural rights that don't require a government or social contract to guarantee, they include civil, political, economic, social, and cultural rights that are subject to whims of the government, and can be instigated, modified, repealed, or restrained at will. These rights are more aspirational in nature and provide suggestions on things that a government should do for its citizens. Depending on your political viewpoints, you may or may not agree with some of the items from the Declaration of Human Rights. It includes well-received ideas like the right not to be tortured, enslaved, or discriminated against. But then it advocates for the right to be employed and paid a living wage, the right to have paid vacations, the right to have sufficient food, clothing, housing, education, and health care, the right to receive financial support if you are poor, elderly, needy, disabled, and so on.

> "Our natural, inalienable rights are now considered to be a dispensation from government, and freedom has never been so fragile, so close to slipping from our grasp as it is at this moment."
>
> —Ronald Reagan

Assignments

✎ 2A: Where do our natural rights come from?

✎ 2B: What should you do if someone or something tries to take away your natural rights?

✎ 2C: Why is the right to own property essential to the free market system?

✎ 2D: What is the biggest difference between an inalienable right and all the other rights?

✎ 2E: What are some government programs that attempt to provide human rights?

✎ 2F: There are additional universal rights that cannot be taken away by government, such as the right to have a family or the right to privacy. Can you think of others?

✎ 2G: What are some other rights that people think are important today, but are not inalienable rights?

Lesson 3

Accept responsibilities

With every right comes a responsibility. Like a coin, you can't pick up one side without picking up the other. Furthermore, the greater the right, the greater the responsibility. Some rights may demand a responsibility that you can't afford to pay by yourself.

- If you want the right to be respected for your individuality, you must accept the responsibility to respect others.
- If you want the right to purchase quality services, you have the responsibility to pay a fair price for those services.
- If you want the right to drive a car, you must drive the car responsibly and lawfully.
- If you want the right to privacy, you must accept the responsibility to give that right to others.
- If you want the right to travel to other countries, you must be willing to obey the laws and respect the folkways of those countries.
- If you want the right to consume addictive drugs, you must be willing to become a slave to those drugs.

Notice that all these rights and responsibilities are based on the principle of reciprocity. Reciprocity is the idea that you agree to exchange things of similar value with others. It is embodied in the concept of karma where your action eventually produces an equal and opposite reaction, when a good deed done now will lead to benefits in the future. This is also taught as the law of the harvest: you only reap what you have sown; don't expect to harvest tomatoes if you only planted squash.

If you want your back to be scratched by someone, then you should be willing to scratch their back. If you want groceries from the store, you need to pay for those groceries. If you want your neighbor to do you a favor, you should be willing to do a favor for your neighbor. If you make charges on a credit card, you must be willing to repay that loan with interest. Forgetting, ignoring, or disregarding to reciprocate, will lead to broken trust, suspension of those rights, and other unpleasant consequences.

Most people understand that nothing in this world is free, that there is always a price to be paid. Freedom from tyrannical or oppressive governments is often purchased with very high prices, often paid with the lives of soldiers and the devastation it brings to their families, their community, and society in general. Too many people who currently live in a state of liberty and enjoy many rights, have no clue as to the price that was paid to secure the rights they inherited. They also don't understand their current responsibilities to maintain those rights.

Freedom is the consequence of paying the price and accepting responsibility for the consequences of your choices. If you do not accept responsibilities, you do not get the freedom unless you go into debt or enslave others to pay the required price.

When governments irresponsibly rack up trillions of dollars of debt to provide unfunded handouts to their citizens, those who financed that money will always want something of greater value in return. How will those debts be paid? It is morally reprehensible to kick the payment down the road and hope our children and grandchildren will pay it. Will it be paid with inflation and skyrocketing prices? With the seizure of personal assets? With the bankruptcy of your business? With unaffordable housing? With regulations that are impossible to comply with? With excessive taxation? With low take-home pay? With the loss of private property? With being sold into bondage or slavery? With imprisonment? With the loss of rights? With war? With the loss of family members? With the loss of your life? Throughout history, these are the ways previous generations paid their debts.

"No man was ever endowed with a right without being at the same time saddled with a responsibility."

—Gerald W. Johnson

Assignments

- 3A: What are some of the duties and responsibilities you shoulder as part of your citizenship?

- 3B: What price are you willing to pay for the rights you enjoy?

- 3C: What responsibilities are the hardest for you to accept?

- 3D: Which debts are you unwilling to pay?

- 3E: What should be done about those who are unwilling to reciprocate?

- 3F: How can you help those who are willing but unable to reciprocate?

Lesson 4

Evaluate consequences

Regardless of where or when we live, each of us are given the freedom to make choices that deliver consequences that impact our lives. If we can't or won't make those decisions on our own, then others will help us make them, which may or may not be in our best interests. Some people may even try to make them for you, cutting you out of the decision-making process entirely. Not everyone does this malevolently, and may even be trying to help you out, but it may deliver consequences that aren't desirable.

> "Between stimulus and response there is a space. In that space is our power to choose our response. In our response lies our growth and our freedom."
>
> —Viktor E. Frankl

Consider what happens when we choose someone to represent us in government. In essence we are delegating to them some of our power so they can act as our proxies and make decisions for us. If they regularly ignore your input and act in ways that you don't approve of, it would be in your best interest to choose a different candidate or run for office yourself, otherwise you get whatever consequences they choose to deliver, whether you like them or not.

We are all affected by the choices of others. Think about a person who chooses to pay more attention to a portable electronic device while driving rather than to the road and its traffic, may unintentionally crash into another vehicle and harm or kill its occupants. While they didn't start out the day with the intention of committing manslaughter, their poor decisions eliminated others from making any choices at all, which will certainly end up imprisoning their body for a while, and their emotional well-being for a long, long while.

Unintended consequences also regularly occur. Consider the plight of honorable veterans who chose to serve their country, but after a tour of duty in an active war zone, return home with an internal battle that continues to rage in their hearts and mind. If they can't choose a constructive way to quell the conflict and find peace, they may choose destructive methods or pick up habits that end up harming relationships instead of enhancing them, bringing even more conflict and chaos into their lives.

The secret to making good decisions is to always be mindful of the consequences that are always associated with a choice. We must take a quick breath and put the consequences of taking an action and not taking an action on a scale and decide which one weighs more. Most of the time we can't see all the consequences, but we should be able to see many of them.

For example, choosing to have an extramarital affair will bring a few minutes of pleasurable satiation to your sexual appetites but will also bring years of painful consequences to your marriage and family that may starve them of the affection and trust they were promised. Is it worth it?

Whenever our animalistic passions surface, our rational thinking often goes into hiding, like a mouse who gets a whiff of a ravenous cat. Learning how to intentionally bridle those intense passions so they can be used in positive rather than negative ways is perhaps the greatest challenge in life. However, it is also the greatest predictor of success, both in your personal life and in your work life.

Learning how to keep your destination in mind and channel your energy into making forward progress, rather than pulling off the road at every roadside attraction or caving into your cravings at every candy shop, will allow you to achieve your ambitions and fulfill your dreams, bringing not only short-term happiness, but long-term happiness as well.

Assignments

🖉 4A: What circumstances cause you to lose the ability to make rational judgments?

🖉 4B: What can you do to stop yourself from making choices without first engaging your brain and evaluating the consequences?

🖉 4C: Some believe that religious commandments or moral laws prohibit their freedoms. Do you agree? Why or why not?

🖉 4D: Can you think of an example where someone has done something that unintentionally affected you in a positive or negative way? Explain.

Lesson 5

Cherish freedom

If we define general freedom as a condition where the average person enjoys a smörgåsbord of political, civil, religious, economic, cultural, educational, legal, social, and personal freedoms, then it is a rare commodity. As far as we can tell, throughout the history of civilization, widespread freedoms have only occurred a few times in a few places for only 250 years at the most. Most people who have lived on this planet have never experienced the breadth or depth of freedoms we now enjoy.

The *Cato Institute* and *Freedom House,* two organizations that measure the amount of freedom in countries and territories throughout the world, report that in the 21st Century, approximately 40% are free, 30% are partly free, and 30% are not free at all. While most nations seem to have some freedoms, there are still too many who don't, and they control the lives of billions of people.

The economic prosperity of a nation is often positively correlated with the amount of freedom its citizens enjoy. The more freedom, the higher the standard of living. Some believe that this isn't just a correlation, but a causation. But which way does the cause flow? Does freedom cause prosperity or does prosperity cause freedom? Whatever your answer is, you should probably be thankful that you are alive at this time in the earth's history and that you have as many freedoms as you do.

Sadly, like most everything in life, people are rarely satisfied with what they currently have. They want more. This compels some to lose their sense of perspective and gratitude, and demand even more entitlements. Funny enough, these demands are usually focused on themselves and their tribe of choice rather than on those who have far fewer freedoms.

This exposes an ugly side of freedom. When you have many freedoms, you also have the responsibility to use those freedoms wisely. Just because you can freely do something, doesn't mean you should. If you use your freedom to tear down your government and the freedoms it secures, then you may lose your freedoms. If you truly believe in the notion of justice, and you use your freedom to trample on the rights of others, don't be surprised if your own rights are trampled on and pared back to the nubbins.

> "Free people, remember this maxim: we may acquire liberty, but it is never recovered if it is once lost."
>
> —Jean-Jacques Rousseau

To cherish something means that we keep it in our minds for a long period of time, not just on national holidays or election days. Cherishing also indicates affection, endearment, and nurturance, which means we will be good stewards of freedom as long as we live, keeping it strong and alive so we can pass it down to future generations just like it was passed to us. We will appreciate it, marvel at it, defend it, show it off, and encourage others to seek for it in their own lives.

Assignments

🖉 5A: Are people more well off because they are more free, or are they more free because they are well off? Explain your answer.

🖉 5B: Would you prefer to be poor and free rather than rich with no liberties? Explain.

🖉 5C: What can you do to help people who have fewer freedoms than you?

🖉 5D: What can you do to gain a greater sense of gratitude and appreciation for the freedoms you enjoy?

Lesson 6

Grant personal freedoms

The better we understand human temperament, the more we realize that an individual's preferences affect just about everything they do in life, including the personal freedoms they want to enjoy as they make their way through life. These are not political freedoms that are granted by governments but are personal freedoms that are granted from an organization to its members or from one individual to another.

> "For to be free is not merely to cast off one's chains, but to live in a way that respects and enhances the freedom of others."
>
> —Nelson Mandela

When personal liberties are acknowledged and granted, and allowed to be freely exercised, it is likely to lead to an increase in personal happiness and satisfaction while simultaneously reducing stress and conflict because we are eliminating the cognitive dissonance that comes when our behaviors can't align with our values. The happier we are, the more productive we tend to be, and the more time we are willing to spend in that setting.

But this necessarily means that different people will have different personal freedoms than others. While some may view this as unfair or biased, isn't it more unfair to treat people uniformly even if they desire to be treated differently? If someone wanted to be called "Andy" but you intentionally ignore them and call them "Andrew," isn't that insensitive? If someone wanted a quiet workspace while someone else wanted a noisy workspace, wouldn't it be unfair to accommodate one person's desires over the other? Because some freedoms are likely to conflict with others, if we universally applied the same freedoms to everyone, whose freedoms would you choose to standardize?

If we are sincerely trying to enhance our relationships and are in a position where we can accommodate someone's preferences, shouldn't we try to do that as often as possible? Sometimes it may not be possible to do it, but if it is, let's do it! In essence, we are giving each temperament their own "safe space" with their own set of permissions that allow them act in ways that accommodate their values and preferences. Imagine what would happen if these colorized freedoms were reciprocally granted to each other in any personal or business relationship, and latitude to exercise these freedoms was encouraged and permanency knitted into the fabric of the relationship.

Below is a list of some of the freedoms that each different temperament appreciates:

Blue Freedoms

- The freedom to build and enhance interpersonal relationships.
- The freedom to conduct activities that build morale and unity.
- The freedom to show empathy and compassion.
- The freedom to broker peace between opponents.
- The freedom to encourage personal growth and well-being.
- The freedom to create a harmonious and comfortable environment.
- The freedom to champion worthwhile causes.

- The freedom to have democratic leadership.
- The freedom to express your uniqueness.
- The freedom to compromise, cooperate, and build consensus.
- The freedom to have conversations and share emotions.
- The freedom to involve feelings in the decision-making process.
- The freedom to promote unity and belonging.

Gold Freedoms

- The freedom to expect follow-through and progress reports.
- The freedom to work the established plan.
- The freedom to fulfill commitments and obligations.
- The freedom to protect and preserve resources.
- The freedom to keep things neat and orderly.
- The freedom to adhere to rules and requirements.
- The freedom to schedule their lives.
- The freedom to be punctual and prepared.
- The freedom to make and keep commitments.
- The freedom to measure worth by completion.
- The freedom to prepare for the future.
- The freedom to be responsible and dedicated.
- The freedom to seek positions of authority.

Green Freedoms

- The freedom to self-correct and self-motivate.
- The freedom to develop more competence.
- The freedom to occasionally skip social events.
- The freedom to identify problems and potential solutions.
- The freedom to formulate logical arguments.

- The freedom to troubleshooting problem areas.
- The freedom to think outside the box.
- The freedom to care about accuracy and precision.
- The freedom to take extra time to make decisions.
- The freedom to encourage concise communication.
- The freedom to look for intellectual stimulation.
- The freedom to give more weight to thought than feelings.
- The freedom to analyze and rearrange systems.

Orange Freedoms

- The freedom to be energetic and competitive.
- The freedom to focus on getting results.
- The freedom to bend rules if necessary.
- The freedom to abbreviate meetings and discussions.
- The freedom to negotiate skillfully.
- The freedom to delegate paperwork.
- The freedom to demonstrate courage in a crisis.
- The freedom to speak boldly and candidly.
- The freedom to tackle challenges head-on.
- The freedom to be spontaneous and flexible.
- The freedom to take risks.
- The freedom to introduce variety into their activities.
- The freedom to be informal and casual.

Assignments

🖉 6A: What freedoms would you like to add to any of the lists above?

🖉 6B: What benefits would you expect to see if we gave each other the freedom to act in a way that maximizes the personal freedoms listed above?

🖉 6C: What challenges do you think might arise if you were to implement this approach?

Introduction

How to enjoy immediacy and living in the moment

Ah, to live in the moment. To be focus on the here and now rather than worrying about what might happen next. This quality could be a virtue, and help prevent too much anxiety from building up, but if you take it to the extreme, it could also become a vice. If you go to a casino and impulsively place your life savings on the roulette wheel, chances are that's not going to end well. So how do we be immediate and yet wise at the same time? Let's find out.

 If you value immediacy, you are present-oriented. You don't fret over the past or map out the future-you focus on what's happening today. You like to keep your options open so you can have the freedom to respond to whatever happens. You enjoy making on-the-spot decisions. Your motto might be, "Just Do It Now!"

Just like every other virtue, there are rules that we must follow if we want to maximize of the benefits of the virtue and minimize its liabilities.

First, we need to master our impulsivity. If you can't control your impulses and they control you, then you are plagued with addictions or compulsions. On the other hand, if you always dismiss or ignore your gut instincts or feelings, you might get pounced on by a stealthy man-eating tiger. Balance is the key.

Second, Get up close and personal. This is the way you communicate and interact with other people. We will reveal some verbal and non-verbal behaviors that will boost your immediacy and create a sense of closeness and togetherness.

Third, control appetites. We'll start out with a little Freudian psychology and learn why our appetites are so powerful and influence our thoughts and behaviors. We will learn how to impose rules, boundaries, and limitations on these appetites so we can achieve our goals.

Fourth, listen to inner voice. We're talking about your conscience here, which is the awareness that helps us make decisions that correlate with our values. Listening to this voice helps us determine right from wrong, good from bad, and virtue from vice.

Fifth, enhance your senses. In this section we won't just talk about the five exteroceptive senses like vision, hearing, touch, taste, and smell. But we'll also examine the interoceptive senses that come from within our bodies and minds. You have more senses than you think you do.

Sixth, improvise your performance. Rarely does life fit into a model of predictable linear progression. Learning how to improvise and "play it by ear" and build upon the contributions of others, will take your ability to live in the present up a notch.

Lesson 1

Master impulsivity

Impulsivity is often defined as the inclination to act on a sudden urge or desire rather than thought. Psychologists describe it as acting on emotion, without forethought or careful consideration of risks and consequences. Both interpretations suggest that acting on your impulses means that you aren't clearly thinking things through or are guilty of leaping before you look. In fact, impulsive acts are often characterized as irrational, reflexive, and stimulus bound. Overall, you walk away from these definitions with the net impression that impulsivity is negative and undesirable when compared with rational thought. That's unfortunate, and is clearly biased towards intellect, because impulsivity, properly mastered, can be strength rather than a weakness.

As with just about everything in life, too much or too little of something is often harmful to yourself and your relationships. If you can't control your impulses and they control you, then you are plagued with addictions or compulsions. On the other hand, if you always dismiss or ignore your gut instincts or feelings, then perhaps you are ignoring a valuable source of information that could have protected you from being pounced on by a stealthy man-eating tiger. Balance is the key to success in life, yet again. Some situations require instincts more than thought, while others require the other. Learning how to differentiate between those circumstances and choose the input source that is more valuable at the time, will go a long way to enhancing your self-mastery. In fact, there are repetitively few circumstances when simultaneously using both clear thinking and feeling-based impressions wouldn't be beneficial. We have a heart and a head for a reason just like we have two legs; one without the other leads to a lifetime of hopping, toppling, and dropping.

> "More errors arise from inhibited indecision than from impulsive behavior."
>
> —Morris L. Ernst

Scientifically, these two mechanisms are called the *impulsive system* and the *reflective system*. The impulsive system delivers fast reactions that are almost automatic in nature and require very little thought or cognitive effort. They are habitual, reflexive, and instinctual, and may be reinforced through repetition and practice. The reflective system is much slower and more deliberate because it takes time to carefully identify choices and evaluate consequences. Medical doctors tell us that if we eat too much, exercise too little, or consume substances that cause more harm than good, then all we need to do is exert conscious reflective control over our habitual, impulsive behaviors—far easier said than done; mindfulness can't be developed overnight.

Assuming it was possible, and we got rid of our impulses entirely, we would quickly wind up in state of mental fatigue or exhaustion. There is simply not enough time in the day to deliberate over every thought and action. Ever tried turning off the medulla at the bottom of your brainstem and using your thoughts to control your heart rhythm, breath rate, blood flow, and body temperature? The simplest task would take an extremely long time to execute. Perhaps someday we can implant some sort of artificial intelligence or neuroenhancement device from Google, Amazon, Microsoft, or Apple that could take over some of our decision-making challenges, but there are too many dystopian and apocalyptic stories that tell us this isn't a good plan at all.

Wouldn't it be better to take the time to develop virtuous habits and patterns of high utility that become so natural and automatic that they seem instinctive or impulsive? Wouldn't it be better to develop knee-jerk reactions that help ourselves and others rather than hurt someone's shins? If we want a happy life, we will systematically replace all of the habits and impulses that hurt or harm with those that enhance and edify.

Assignments

✎ 1A: What are some impulses and instincts that have produced negative results in your life?

✎ 1B: What are some impulses and instincts that have produced positive results in your life?

✎ 1C: What role does immediate impulse have in creativity?

✎ 1D: How will you get rid of negative impulses and replace them with more positive impulses?

Lesson 2

Get up close and personal

Another aspect of immediacy is the way you communicate and interact with other people. Social psychologist Albert Mehrabian is best known for work on how to improve the congruence between verbal and nonverbal communications to ensure you are using both forms to communicate the same message, such as not saying, "Yes" while your head is wagging, "No." In fact, he attributes that up to 55% of a message is delivered through facial expressions, with tone of voice representing 38%, and the actual words a mere 7%. This gives credence to the sentiment that "how" you say something is more important than "what" you say.

> "People are drawn toward persons and things they like, evaluate highly, and prefer; and they avoid or move away from things they dislike, evaluate negatively, or do not prefer."
>
> —Albert Mehrabian

For communication to be effective, he suggests that you invoke the "principle of immediacy," which essentially means to shorten the distance between someone when you communicate with them. Move in or lean in closer, being careful not to invade their personal space, which is a bubble about 1.5 to 3 feet away (it varies by culture and temperament). Then watch to see what they do. If the person takes a step away from you, they may not enjoy such close proximities at this point in time, if so, give them their space. People tend to avoid or move away from things they dislike, evaluate negatively, or distrust. Your job is to now build up that trust and ameliorate their concerns. One of the best ways to do that is to create the impression that right now, out of all the people that exist in the world, they are the center of your universe and deserve your full attention.

By creating a sense of closeness or togetherness with someone, it conveys the message that you are comfortable with that person, you like them to one degree or another, you are interested in what they have to say, and you intend to be close enough so you can pay attention to both their verbal and nonverbal messages. Once someone trust you, moving in or leaning in almost always received favorably and is an act of friendship. This physical immediacy or closeness needs to exist in all your face-to-face communications, not just with friends or family. If you want to convey honesty, concern, and a willingness to discuss things, even difficult things, move in. Don't hide behind an object, like a desk or a phone. If you need to, start off sitting side-by-side if it is too awkward or uncomfortable to sit knee to knee.

Verbal immediacy boosters

- Call them by name.
- Be informal and casual.
- Refer to their good qualities.
- Express your positive views of the person.
- Express appreciation for your relationship.
- Encourage them to continue, such as: "And then what happened?"
- Give appropriate verbal feedback.
- Use terms like "we" and "us."
- Talk about things you have in common.
- Disclose something significant about yourself.

Non-verbal immediacy boosters

- Arrange your body to exclude third parties.
- Maintain comfortable eye contact.
- Use appropriate levels of touch.
- Maintain a relaxed body posture.
- Avoid ambiguous, meaningless gestures.
- Smile with your eyes and mouth.
- Use vocal variety; avoid a monotone voice.
- Intentionally show emotions on your face.
- Maintain appropriate eye contact.
- Limit looking around at other things or people.
- Give appropriate non-verbal feedback.
- Maintain physical closeness.
- Don't look at the time.

Assignments

✎ 2A: What benefits will you receive by communicating with more immediacy?

✎ 2B: What gets in your way when you try to get closer to others?

✎ 2C: What is your personal space threshold? Ask your friends or family about their bubble size. What is the average distance before it gets too close or too far away?

✎ 2D: Sometimes people who trust and like you may not be in the mood for a close conversation. How can you tell if this is the case?

Lesson 3

Control appetites

According to the founder of psychoanalysis, Sigmund Freud, the human psyche is composed of three components: the id, the *ego,* and the *superego.*

The instinctual id component seeks out the immediate gratification of all our needs, wants, and urges—regardless of the consequences. It tries to fulfill our most basic and primitive appetites and desires, including hunger, thirst, sex, and elimination, and treats with aggression anything that prevents those things from happening. If our needs go unfulfilled, and we don't experience pleasure, then, according to Freud, we experience anxiety, tension, and a variety of mental disorders.

To control the powerful id, Freud explained that the ego aspect of our personality tries to satisfy the id's desires in realistic and socially acceptable ways, usually through the delayed gratification process where we wait until an appropriate time and place to privately satiate our needs and desires. It understands that you are a member of a society and if you don't act in ways that the society has established, you will be cast out of that society. In essence, the id is the horse, and the ego is the horse's rider. The more educated but less powerful rider controls the movements of the horse, reins in its passions, leads it bit by bit, and spurs the horse forward when necessary.

But which direction does the horse and its rider go? What is their destination? That's the function of the super ego or "conscience" which helps us internalize moral standards, values, ethics, and ideals that we have acquired throughout our life, such as those embraced by our parents and culture. It provides the sense of right and wrong which guides the ego as it makes judgments and steers the horse. It is this aspect of our personality that compels us to adhere to basic rules and standards and makes us more civil and virtuous. It is what makes an ideal society possible.

Now whether you agree with Freud's tripartite theory of personality or not, the idea of a "pleasure principle" which drives us to immediately satiate our desires, regardless of the consequences, seems to be the dominating force in an increasingly number of people. As a society, if we have gotten into the habit of ignoring the ego's "don't do that in public" tactic or the super-ego's "that isn't right, don't do it at all" advice, then all we have left is the id whose sole purpose of existence is to spend, eat, drink, and be merry for tomorrow we die. This myopic philosophy, as history has repeated shown, always leads to incivility, selfishness, anarchy, nihilism, and the collapse of a cooperative, tolerant, virtuous, and self-governing society. If there is no absolute moral truth, then why not break the laws, rack up debts, loot what you want, threaten your neighbors, drive while under the influence, destroy your enemies, kill off the undesirables, and have sex with anything that moves or doesn't move?

Assuming you're still reading, and aren't off partying like there's no tomorrow, then let us vow to seize more control over our appetites so that we can maintain some level of balance, decency, decorum, and civility within ourselves. Hopefully, we will surround ourselves with others who champion similar beliefs and values so that we can interact safely and thrive, rather than merely survive. There is a time and a place for everything, including satiating our physical appetites and desires, but they should be governed, not left unattended to roam the range freely, tromping down the crops of your neighbor and wrecking relationships in their wake. All cravings, just like all attitudes and behaviors, should be given rules, boundaries, and limitations so that we can achieve our goals, including the goal to systematically abandon vice and replace it with virtue.

"One might compare the relation of the ego to the id with that between a rider and his horse. The horse provides the locomotor energy, and the rider has the prerogative of determining the goal and of guiding the movements of his powerful mount towards it. But all too often in the relations between the ego and the id we find a picture of the less ideal situation in which the rider is obliged to guide his horse in the direction in which it itself wants to go."

—Sigmund Freud

Assignments

- 3A: When any of Freud's three elements of the psyche get out of balance with the others, bad attitudes and behaviors start emerging. For example, what happens if you have a superego that is too dominant? What would you expect to see?

- 3B: Maturity is learning to endure the pain of deferred gratification. Explain why you agree or disagree with this statement.

- 3C: Is there anything wrong with pursuing pleasure first and trying to avoid unpleasure? Shouldn't we look for situations with the least pain and stress? Explain your thoughts.

- 3D: What kind of negative behaviors do you see when controlling appetites becomes too difficult to manage on our own? Where can we turn to for help?

- 3E: Which appetites do you have the easiest time controlling? The hardest time controlling?

- 3F: What benefits do you stand to gain by taking more control of your appetites?

Lesson 4

Listen to inner voice

The word *conscience* comes from two Latin words that mean "knowing with." It is the awareness of the self that makes decisions based on values. It is that faculty of our mind that helps us determine right from wrong, good from bad, virtue from vice. It is what compels us to feel guilty or remorseful when we do something bad, or happy and satisfied when we do something good. It usually appears unexpectedly as a sudden insight or flash of inspiration that compels you into taking an immediate positive action.

While Freud called it the superego, most modern psychologists describe it as your conscience or inner voice. Some secularists refer to it as your intuition or your sixth sense. Christians christen it the light of Christ or the voice of God that is felt in your heart in heard in your mind. Hindus call it the sacred knowledge you have learned about good and evil. Muslims call it the voice calling you to follow the struggle of goodness over evil as taught by Muhammad. Buddhists call it an unselfish love for all life that comes through a gradual enlightenment. Judaism says it is the truth revealed through God-given laws. Almost every religion has some sort of corollary for the conscience whose function is to help us live good, peaceful, and fulfilling lives.

Our conscience usually manifests itself through thoughts or feelings that come to us when we face a decision, big or small. It is always edifying, enlightening, and encourages you to do something good. It is often experienced immediately, like an impulse, as we judge our options. Some people report it as a quiet, whispering voice even though it doesn't generate sound that is processed through our auditory system. Like sound, it appears we can become deaf to it if we intentionally filter it out or ignore it long enough. It seems to be heard or felt not within a physical body, but within what some describe as your inner spirit or life force, which is like the unseen hand moving within an external physical glove. According to many faith traditions, when you are conceived, that spirit enters your physical body and you become a living soul; when you die, that spirit leaves your physical body but continues to exist on a transcendental plane where it is still influenced by your conscience.

Now whether this grossly simplified interpretation of human existence rings true to your conscience or not, it still has relevance because billions of your fellow earth dwellers believe it to be true. They hope, for the sake of humanity and a peaceful, fair-minded, co-existence, that you will regularly choose right over wrong, good over evil, righteousness over wickedness. But they will not compel you to obey your conscience—that is entirely your prerogative. You are the one who must live with the consequences of your choices, and hopefully, those consequences won't harm too many innocent bystanders.

> "A good conscience is to the soul what health is to the body; it preserves constant ease and serenity within us; and more than countervails all the calamities and afflictions which can befall us from without."
>
> —Joseph Addison

Assignments

🖉 4A: What is your understanding about the human conscience?

🖉 4B: If you think it is real, how has it been manifested to you?

🖉 4C: When you receive a clear impression from out of the blue to do something, and it entices you to do something good, it is likely from your conscience. What if it entices you to do something bad? Should you still follow that prompting? Why or why not?

Lesson 5

Enhance your senses

Aristotle put forth the hypothesis that humans only have five senses: vision, hearing, touch, taste, and smell. According to modern scientists, he was a little off. Those five senses are now known as exteroceptive senses that carry information about the external world. But what about the internal world of our body and mind? These are called interoceptive sensors, such as the senses that detect pleasure, pain, temperature, balance, acceleration, muscle stretch, blood pressure, blood oxygen content, lung inflation, full stomach, and bladder stretch—just to name a few.

Furthermore, each of our senses can be broken down into subsenses. For example, we have at least five different flavors for taste: sweet, salt, sour, bitter, and the savory umami. But what about the temperature of that food or drink? Don't our tongues also let us know if something is too hot or too cold? Or wet? Or sticky? What happens when we combine multiple senses together? Do they form new senses?

Can we sense in others fear or danger, as well as uncertainty or insincerity? And what about our temporal senses that detect the passage of time? Or the ones that tell us where are body parts are at any given moment? And how can we forget about the extra-sensory perceptions like near-death experiences, déjà vu, second sight, clairvoyance, or precognition that take the form of dreams, visions, or prophecies that later come true?

People who live in the present, rely on their senses to deliver accurate information so that they can make good decisions. If you're roaming around Yellowstone National Park looking for place to go skinny-dipping, and you stumble across a colorful hot spring that has steam rising from it and you smell something akin to rotten eggs, if your senses of sight and smell aren't functioning properly, and you ignore the posted signs as well as that warning bell blaring in your conscience, you might jump into some scalding, caustic, toxic soup. As you're recovering in the hospital's burn unit, you might as well also get your common sense checked out—it may need resuscitation.

> "Variety's the very spice of life, that gives it all its flavor."
>
> —William Cowper

As we get older, we can expect to see some decline in our senses, especially hearing and vision, just like we see decline in all our other body parts and passions. Around age 60, our 10,000 taste buds start to shrink, making it difficult to differentiate different flavors. Around age 70, our sense of smell starts to diminish. Of course, if we have been exposed to toxic chemicals, have regularly ingested toxins like nicotine, caffeine, alcohol, and other harmful substances, or have contracted at least one physical disease, we often see earlier degradation. Adopting a healthier lifestyle will delay this process a bit, but sooner or later it all goes to pot.

Regardless of your age, if you feel like your senses could use a little tune-up, researchers tell us they can be enhanced a bit. This involves exposing a sense to an expanded variety of conditions and trying to differentiate those differences. For example, you can sniff a variety of different fragrances until you learn how to pick up on subtle differences. Or you can refine your taste palette by sampling a wide assortment of cheeses, wines, or ice creams. Or perhaps you sprinkle your food with one of the hundreds of different herbs or spices that exist in the world.

Just like muscles get flabby without regular exercise, so do your senses. Eating the same thing day after day dulls your tastes, being exposed to the same light day after day affects your eyesight, listening to the same type of music is not only boring, but leads you to ignore other genres that might be worth hearing.

While Aristotle may have been slightly off in his understanding of human senses, modern science has revealed that our senses are even more complex than originally thought. Our senses not only detect external information, but also internal information about our bodies and minds. As we age, our senses may decline, but there are ways to enhance and improve them through exposure to a variety of stimuli. Keeping our senses sharp is important for making good decisions and experiencing the richness and variety of life.

Assignments

🖉 5A: What senses would you like to enhance?

🖉 5B: How can enhancing your senses allow you to enjoy living in the moment?

🖉 5C: Why are some people afraid to explore the world with their senses.

Lesson 6

Improvise your performance

To "play it by ear" means that you can play an instrument without needing music notation. While it may seem magical on the surface to those who haven't studied music, in reality it is the result of learnable musical skills such as music theory and familiarity with your instrument. Unless you are tone deaf and can't differentiate notes from each other, you can learn to play by ear in five or six months. In fact, it is a valuable skill for musicians who may need to perform without notice or advanced preparation. While learning how to play by ear may be useful, it isn't as nearly as useful as its metaphor. To "play it by ear" means you can immediately assess a situation and act spontaneously in helpful and proactive ways. It means you have no game plan except to tap into your reservoir of knowledge, experience, and skills and hope you emerge safely on the other side.

Rarely does life fit into a model of predictable linear progression. While we work on achieving our plans and goals, someone or something always comes at us out of nowhere and threatens to take us off track. The trick is to be able to handle those temporary interruptions and jump through any hoops it left behind. Adaptability is a virtue that was discussed elsewhere in this material which teaches us how to be more flexible and make course adjustments as needed. But what we are talking about now is the ability to improvise and take immediate action.

To help us learn how to improvise we can examine the comedic art of improvisation. If you've watched live ensemble productions such as *Saturday Night Live, The Second City,* or *Whose Line Is It Anyway,* you've seen scenic improvisation at work. If two actors are on stage, one actor says something, then the next actor builds on it and throws it back to the first actor, who build on the last idea, and the cycle continues. If done well, hilarity ensues; if done poorly, it becomes agonizing to watch.

But it isn't as whimsical as it sounds. According to Kelly Leonard and Tom Yordon, leaders of The Second City organization, improv actors are following a simple formula. If they religiously stick to it, they will be more successful than not. And here is the formula: always say, "Yes, and."

This means you never contradict or ignore what the previous performer said, you always agree with it and then add to it. "Yes, but" is a form of negation and must be avoided, as is "No, but." In improv, you must work together to reach the end of the scene. Saying, "Yes," builds that togetherness, and the "and" part moves the dialog forward. If you try to force the dialog to move in a particular direction or hog the scene, it destroys trust and camaraderie. Everyone on the improv team is on the same stage, with no leaders and no specialists. Everyone is equal and takes their turn with their own unique spin.

For an improv session to be successful, you must constantly focus on the other people on your team, carefully listening and paying attention to everything going on around you, from words, to gestures, to facial expressions. Your role is to build on the words and actions of others; to be constructive rather than destructive. Sometimes it won't pan out as expected, and might even end in a spectacular failure, but don't let the fear of failure stop you from acting. This is a team effort after all, so a failure for one is a failure for all. Please keep in mind that failure is a part of progression; without failure we would never improve. So, fail with confidence!

This idea of working on a team and always saying, "Yes, and" isn't limited to what you see at a comedy club, it also can be used in your business teams and personal relationships, in fact, anytime you find yourself working with someone else, especially when you are trying to brainstorm new solutions to old problems. Imagine what would happen if everyone took turns contributing small ideas and then explored ways to make them fit in with other small ideas. If everyone worked together, it would eventually amount to a big idea. At the end of the day, it may be a horrible idea, but it would be a team failure, not a personal one. You are all in this together. You can spin out a different idea tomorrow. The most important thing is not necessarily solving the problem but building relationships that can give you the resilience and support system to weather and solve all problems.

To recap, the key to successful improvisation and thinking on your feet, is to spread the solution development work across your team, where everyone contributes with a "Yes, and" attitude and all share credit or blame for the outcomes.

> "Improvisation means coming to the situation without rigid expectations or preconceptions. The key to improvisation is motion—you keep going forward, fearful or not, living from moment to moment. That's how life is."
>
> —Bobby McFerrin

Assignments

🖉 6A: Test out your improvisation skills by pairing up with someone and having a conversation without using the word I. What does it take to be successful at this task?

🖉 6B: The next time you are sitting with a handful of friends or family around a table, create a story where each person contributes one word at a time, with the story progressing around the table one word at a time. Let this go on to develop a story that lasts for several minutes. Does it produce a more interesting story than one you could produce on your own?

🖉 6C: What benefits do you think you could receive by using the "Yes, and" approach in your relationships?

Introduction

Strategies for making a lasting impact on the world

Impact is the desire to have a significant effect on others through both word and deed is a not-so-secret dream of many. To be an influencer, to inspire others, to make a difference in the world—these things are appealing. So how do we go about making an impact on the world? Where should we start? What skills do we need? Let's find out, shall we?

 If you are an impactful person, you are able to do whatever it takes-whatever works-to get the job done, even if that means making mistakes, bending rules, or stepping on toes. You are interested in delivering an intense punch, knocking out the competition, and moving on to new challenges.

If you are an impactful person, you are able to do whatever it takes—whatever works—to get the job done, even if that means making mistakes, bending rules, or stepping on toes. You are interested in delivering an intense punch, knocking out the competition, and moving on to new challenges.

How do we get there from here? How do we become more powerful and influential? Here are six basic steps that will get you pointed in the right direction.

First, identify your friends. In the world of social media, "followers" are the people who want to hear what you have to say.

But followers are not the same as friends. The more intimate you are with your friends, the more time you spend with them, the more influence you have with them. We'll learn how to identify how much influence you may already wield.

Second, extend your sphere of influence. What are you currently doing in the world of social media to influence others? What are some different avenues you can pursue?

Third, get stuff done. Impactful people are known for having the energy and drive to get things done at a pace that eludes most of us. They often have very long lists of things to do and are eager to get work done. What gets in your way and prevents you from making daily progress towards getting what you want most in life?

Fourth, develop more charisma. This magnetism that draws people to you can be acquired by anyone if they really want it. It only takes four steps. You'll discover those in the reading assignments.

Fifth, make a colorful first impression. When you talk with others, make sure you take their temperament into consideration, because each color wants to hear different things from you in an honest and sincere manner.

And sixth, assess your impact. For this step, you will want to use both qualitative and quantitative analysis to measure your impact. To do that you will have to determine what impact would want to make and figure out how you will know when you've reached that goal.

If you're ready to be a mover and a shaker, to become a genuine influencer who helps to make some part of the world a little bit better—then join me as we try to acquire this virtue.

Lesson 1

Identify your friends

In the world of social media, "followers" are the people who want to hear what you have to say. You are called an "influencer" because you have some degree of power over how your followers spend their time as they choose to watch your videos or read your posts. Whether you're providing entertainment, edification, or education, what you do impacts what they think, how they feel, and how they act. But followers are not the same as friends. Friends are people with whom you have a reciprocal relationship, where you regularly spend time with each other in face-to-face interactions. The more intimate you are with your friends, the more time you spend with them, the more influence you have with them.

But how many friends can a person have? According to evolutionary anthropologist Robin Dunbar, there is a correlation between the volume of your brain's neocortex that sits just above your eye sockets and the number of stable relationships you can maintain at any given time. Dunbar's number is 150 social connections on average, give or take 50 or so, but it varies from person to person based on temperament, gender, social skills, and ability to interact. Apparently, our brains simply can't keep track of much more than that, nor is there enough time in your day to maintain those associations. The closer someone is to you, the more time you spend with them, the stronger your ties, the more trust and obligation you feel, and the more intimate and influential your relationship. This is illustrated on the following diagram:

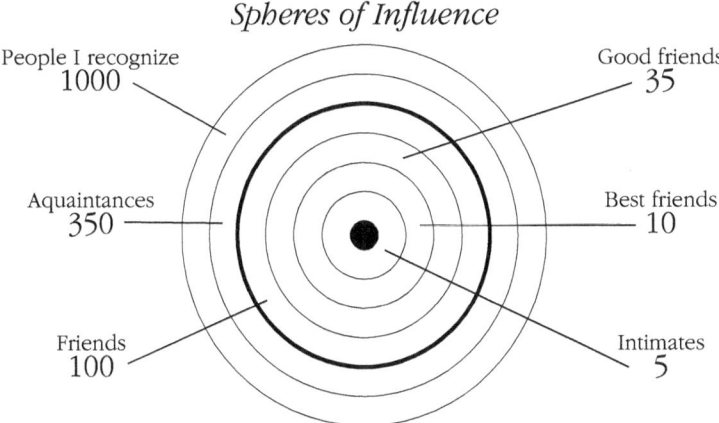

Spheres of Influence

The diagram shows six different categories of associations. Keep in mind that these are average numbers, and your numbers may be different. Starting with you in the middle and working outwards, most people have around five intimate relationships at any given time, which for many people is their family. In order to fit into this category, you need to spend time with them every week, in fact, more than 60% of your social time is devoted to these people. Next, you have 10 others that you would consider to be your best friends with whom you associate at least once a month, perhaps going out to eat, playing games, or just hanging out together. This group could include non-relatives or more of your kinfolk. Next, there are 35 others who you would call your good friends, whom you would invite to a house party or hang out with once every three or four months. And the remaining 100 slots are distant friends with whom you would see once a year or at weddings and funerals. All together that brings the total to around 150 people with whom you have friendships. Beyond that, in the outer two rings, are your acquaintances and then those people to whom you can match a name with a face.

Dunbar's magic number appears to hold true in other aspects of life. Whenever people need to cooperate or perform together to survive, you will see around 150 people in that group. For example, prehistoric hunter-gatherer clans, agricultural villages who barter with each other, and the number of active members of a church parish, all contain around 150 people. If you're planning a wedding party, if you are like the average couple, you might invite around 150 people. If you are a member of the military throughout the world, the smallest self-reliant group is sometimes called a "company" which has an average range of 150 members. In businesses, 150 is about the optimal size of a factory or office building where everyone knows each other and can maintain a sense of common purpose.

Not all researchers agree with Dunbar's findings, suggesting that there isn't a magic number at all. However, the classification of your family and friends into concentric circles based on familiarity and intimacy does allow us to identify those we are more likely to influence because of our deeper relationships.

> "Our social networks can have dramatic effects on our lives. Your chances of becoming obese, giving up smoking, being happy or depressed, or getting divorced are all influenced by how many of your close friends do these things."
>
> —Robin Dunbar

Assignments

✏ 1A: Define your spheres of influence by sorting your friends and loved ones into the various relationship rings defined by Dunbar. You may want to draw a chart like the one above and place their names in it. You may want to keep this list private lest you offend someone who didn't make the cut into a particular group.

✏ 1B: On social media platforms, if you are a typical user, you may have around 350 "friends", but how many do you really care about? And how many do you interact with?

✏ 1C: Besides friendships, can you think of other entities that follow the Dunbar's groupings?

Lesson 2

Extend your influence

For decades, Rupert Murdoch was a heavyweight media mogul. He owned newspapers, magazines, television networks, radio stations, film studios, satellite networks, major internet sites, publishing houses, outdoor advertising companies, and other media venues throughout the world. Like his arch-nemesis, Ted Turner, he had tremendous influence over what more than a billion people saw and heard daily. His control over the media gave him great power. As a result, while not a politician, he routinely met with geopolitical leaders to create policies and programs that shaped entire nations.

Chances are we will never become as wealthy or as powerful as Murdoch, Turner, or one of the media magnates from yesteryear, such as William Hearst or Lord Northcliffe. But we can expand our influence and impact in similar ways on a significantly smaller scale. We can become mini social media moguls by taking advantage of internet sites that deliver different media types to the people we want to influence.

For every traditional media outlet, such as a television station, newspaper, publishing house, or radio station, there is there is a corresponding site on the internet. Twitter, for example, is a billboard, flashing your 140-character tweet to thousands of followers every day. Some of those followers actively seek out your daily tweets as they speed by on the information superhighway, but most don't. Most are simply traveling to a different destination and may or may not notice your billboard flashing its short message. But occasionally, they'll glance over and see something that interests them, something that might even motivate them to action. And that's the goal, isn't it?

The diagram below outlines a typical social media solar system. It shows a central orb surrounded by a number of orbiting satellites. The central orb is your personal newspaper where you spend most of your time. It is where people go if they are interested in news about you, your thoughts on politics and religion, your opinions, your sports and hobbies, your family, your humor, and so on. This is where they can learn everything you want them to know about you.

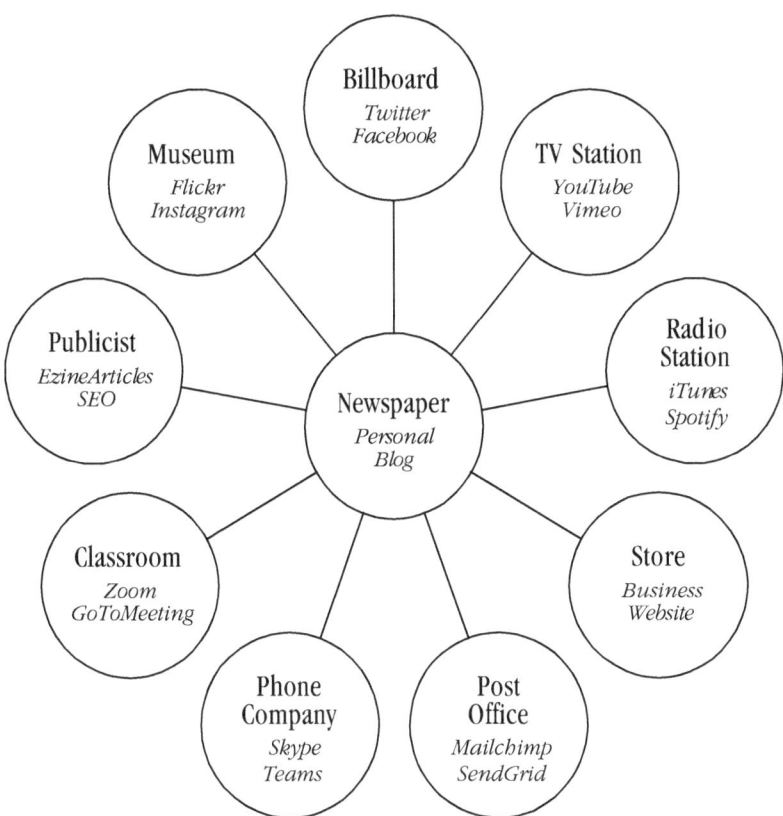

Notice that each satellite is a different media outlet. Your radio station is an audio podcast, housed at iTunes or an internet-radio site. Your television station is located at YouTube or a similar video-hosting service. Skype is your telephone company, allowing you to reach out and touch someone anywhere on the planet. And the correlations go on and on. For every traditional media outlet, there is—or soon will be—an internet equivalent.

People may be introduced to you through one of your satellites, but your prime objective is to get them to visit your home world. Once they land on your blog site, they'll find links to all your satellite sites and will be able to see your world the way you want them to see it.

One of these links may be to your online store where you will give them the opportunity to buy something from you (or one of your affiliates). But it is simply a satellite. You don't want to offend the visitors to your home world by constantly trying to sell something to them. You want to build a long-term relationship with them, where they can learn to know you, like what you are saying, and trust you. If, and only if, you have that relationship established, then visitors will be far more likely to link over to your business site and hand over their money.

Why do we want to seek out and maintain a presence on all these internet-based media outlets? Because that is where the populace assembles and mingles with other people. If you want to be a mover and a shaker, you need to get your message out to as many people as you can. When newer internet sites become more popular than older sites, you'll want to establish a presence there as well. If you, and your solar system, go where the people are going, you'll invariably find more prospects, clients, friends, and followers than you will drifting in the outer darkness of deep space.

"We have technology, finally, that for the first time in human history allows people to really maintain rich connections with much larger numbers of people."

—Pierre Omidyar

Assignments

🖉 2A: Who are some people or organizations on the internet who have been an influence on your life?

🖉 2B: What are you currently doing in the world of social media to try to influence others?

🖉 2C: If you do not want to become a social media mogul, what else can you do to extend your influence?

Lesson 3

Get stuff done

Because they are interested in making a difference in the world, impactful people are known for having the energy and drive to get things done at a pace that eludes most of us. They often have very long lists of things to do and are eager to get work done. To help them stay organized and not waste time, they often spend a little time each morning reviewing the day's upcoming tasks. If a complex or cumbersome scheduling or calendaring system gets in the way, it is thrown out like last night's fries. When it comes to organizing and prioritizing their tasks, they choose systems that are simple and easy to implement.

For example, strategist Bill Westerman developed a quick and dirty task management system that only requires a notebook and a pen or pencil. Every day, he sits down, turns to a blank page, puts the date at the top, and makes a brain dump of all the things that need to be done. The key is to make sure everything on the list is actionable and specific. He then scans through the previous day's list and finds the things that weren't finished and moves them to this page. He then scans through the list and marks the 3–4 items which are most urgent. He uses the notation in the graphic below to indicate if it urgent, if it was moved to another page, if it was completed, or if it was cancelled. Once the prioritized tasks are done, he goes back through and chooses new prioritized tasks. If he does a task but it requires additional follow-up, he adds another box to it. Throughout the day, if a new task comes to mind, he jots it down but doesn't start working on it until the urgent tasks are finished. This method is not only simple, but it also provides a great historical record of accomplishments.

☐ a task
⊡ an urgent task
▨ task moved to another page
☑ completed task
☒ cancelled task
☐-☑ task with a follow-up

If using pen and paper are too old-fashioned for you, you can try one of the hundreds of apps that are available for your computer or phone; there are no shortage of digital solutions. The trick is to find the one that works best for you and your workflow.

To get things done, make sure you divide up your big tasks into smaller tasks, prioritize your list, delegate out the things you don't need to do yourself, eliminate distractions, and focus all your energy on the task at hand. If you have the tendency to procrastinate, make sure you do the things you hate first that way you can spend the rest of the day doing the things you like.

> "There are the few who make things happen; the many more who watch things happen and the overwhelming majority who have no notion of what happened."
>
> —Nicholas M. Butler

Assignments

✏ 3A: What reasons have you seen for why people don't accomplish what they hope to do?

✏ 3B: What gets in your way and prevents you from making daily progress towards getting what you want most in life?

✏ 3C: Why does using a task management system help you accomplish more?

Lesson 4

Develop more charisma

Have you ever walked into a room of people where a particular individual was clearly the center of attraction? They weren't necessarily someone special or important, they just appeared to have a magnetic attraction that placed them smack dab in the middle of the spotlight. People's eyes were glued to them, and when they spoke, time stood still, and everyone listened. Sort of like the late 1970s television commercial for the E.F. Hutton investment firm where an entire room suddenly went silent and leaned in so they could hear the broker's advice. This ability is often called *charisma*, which has been mistakenly attributed to some sort of inborn characteristics—you either have it or you don't. But that's not accurate. Charisma is something that can be acquired by anyone if they want it. It only takes four steps: be present, be confident, be friendly, and be engaging.

First, you need to be fully present in the moment. You must pay attention to everything, taking in the sights and sounds of your environment, understanding where everyone is and what they are doing. You need to send out clear and strong verbal and non-verbal signals that you are fully engaged and excited to be there, even if you are the biggest introvert in the world and would rather be hiding in the corner. If you are talking with someone, make sure it appears as though they have your complete attention. Your body language should constantly indicate enthusiasm, interest, openness, and a desire for emotional connections. Genuine smiles and lots of eye contact are imperative.

Second, you need to remove any self-doubts or self-imposed barriers that might be lingering in your mind. You must feel like you belong and have something to contribute. Set aside your shyness and nervousness. If you feel like you aren't worthy to be in the spotlight, you won't even make it on to the stage. It may help to remember that you possess special powers. We're not talking about your superpowers, like turning invisible or leaping from building to building, but those almost super-human strengths and skills that you've acquired throughout your life and that are inherent within your temperament. Remind yourself that you possess an immensely unique combination of talents, skills, and gifts that can make a significant difference in the lives of those around you. Let that inner confidence shine. It shouldn't make you appear cocky or arrogant, but poised and prepared.

Third, while you're shining with confidence, if you're not a Blue who automatically emanates warmth and amiability, you might need to stoke up those friendly fires within you so that others can sense your sociability, the degree of your passion, and feel your positive energy. It should radiate through your poise, gestures, and every word you speak. It sends out good vibes that you are worthy of their time and attention, can be trusted, and would make a good friend.

Fourth, you need to figure out how to captivate your audience like an actor on a stage. Knowing what we do about human temperament, if we are talking to multiple people, and we are unsure of their colors, we should say things that would appeal, at some point, to the values and preferences of each type. When we tick off those boxes, and weave together an interesting and compelling narrative, imbued with drama, humor, emotion, suspense, and insights, you will find that people enjoy hearing what you say. It doesn't have to be a canned speech, primed to be delivered at the perfect moment, but it should be intentionally engaging, dynamic, and inspiring so that you can make an impact in their lives.

"We need less posturing and more genuine charisma. Charisma was originally a religious term, meaning 'of the spirit' or 'inspired.' It's about letting God's light shine through us. It's about a sparkle in people that money can't buy. It's an invisible energy with visible effects. To let go, to just love, is not to fade into the wallpaper. Quite the contrary, it's when we truly become bright. We're letting our own light shine."

—Marianne Williamson

Assignments

✎ 4A: Do you know someone who seems full of charisma? What makes them so appealing?

✎ 4B: Most people with charisma aren't expert in all four areas, but perhaps two or three. Which aspects would you like to work on? How will you do that?

✎ 4C: Role play with someone who can help you practice engaging conversations. Rehearse as needed until it becomes second nature.

✎ 4D: Why is it important to remember that charisma isn't about hogging the spotlight but shining the spotlight on others, engaging their hearts and minds, and empowering them with the ability to make positive changes?

Lesson 5

Make a colorful first impression

Those who make the most positive impact in the world all share one characteristic: from the very first time you meet them, they are completely honest and only represent what they believe to be true. They are sincere and worthy of trust. On the other hand, those who make the most negative impact, and cause the most disruption and destruction, are those who use dishonesty to manipulate you into taking an action that usually benefits them at your expense. Therefore, if you want to be a positive influence for good and make a difference in the world then honesty must be your defining feature. Once that baseline is established, we can then turn to our understanding of temperament to address one of the next most important characteristics of influencers, which is the ability to appeal to all four types.

> "You never know when a moment and a few sincere words can have an impact on a life."
>
> —Zig Ziglar

Blues will want to believe that you have their best interests at heart. If they get a whiff of insincerity or get an inkling that you are merely pretending to be helpful, then you can kiss that relationship goodbye. You must demonstrate to them that you are trying to make an impact because you truly care. Your motivation comes from your heart and is driving you to take a stand for the good. If what you can do will enhance their relationships with others, you've got a winning proposition. As you try to influence them, you will need to as kind, compassionate, patient, and as thoughtful as you can be.

Golds will want to know if you and your claims are reliable and will do what you say they will do. Trust is a big deal for them, and if you do anything that appears that you aren't reliable or will do what you say you will do, then that's a red flag. They also want information presented to them in a professional, step-by-step manner with guarantees, warrantees, and endorsements from trusted third-party sources. If you are promising more status, security, or sense of control, they will sign the contract.

Greens wants to know about if you and your ideas have been scientifically tested and generate the results you indicate. This means you will need documentation and proof, with spec sheets and data. They may want to know your sources and credentials, and if you can competently answer their questions. They are most influenced by intelligent and knowledgeable people, who can explain pros and cons in an objective, efficient manner, not getting too wrapped up in emotionality or insignificant opinions. They value expertise, so if you can deliver that, you've hooked your Greens.

Oranges are all about results. More than the other types, you need to make sure the presentation is interactive and interesting, and as candid and bold as possible. Oranges are good at what they do and expect you to be good at what you, which at the moment, means you are trying to get them to do something that will create a strong impact in their lives, and perhaps allow them to knock out their competition. It helps if you are outgoing, energetic, and self-assured, while targeting specific benefits that will take the Orange to new heights and new adventures. They are especially appreciative if you have already been down the road yourself and can regale them with your tales, so don't hesitate to offer to mentor them if they want one-on-one help.

So, if you want to make a difference with all four types, make sure within the first minute or so, you build on a foundation of honesty, and then demonstrate sincerity, compassion, reliability, professionalism, trustworthiness, capability, intelligence, credibility, enthusiasm, experience, and boldness. The more of these qualities you portray, and the sooner you do it, the more likely you are to increase your influence. Often the first impression someone has about you, which is formed in less than a minute, may determine whether you will be given the chance to make an impact.

Assignments

🖊 5A: What is it about someone that makes a good impression on you?

🖊 5B: Why is it faster and easier to make an impact on someone if you can figure out their temperament?

🖊 5C: What will you do to elevate your first impressions, both in person and on any social media platform?

Lesson 6

Assess your impact

How do you know if you're making an impact in someone's life? Researchers will tell you that there are basically two types of analysis that can be performed: qualitative and quantitative.

Subjective qualitative research is concerned with figuring out how people describe something through their unique perspective. Usually these thoughts, feelings, and interpretations cannot be measured or compared because they vary from person to person. Qualitative data usually involves non-numerical, interpretative data such as language analysis, interview transcriptions, behavioral observations, and looking for themes or trends.

On the other hand, the objective quantitative method deals with measurements such as quantity, amounts, strength, intensity, capacity, and so on. It assumes that if something can be measured on a fixed scale, then you can give it a numerical value that allows you to make comparisons, predictions, and evaluate it with statistical analysis. It gathers facts and figures that define a highly probable, unchangeable reality.

One method isn't necessarily better than another, and like most things in life, finding the balance between the two is often the best course. Many people start with qualitative research to identify general issues and behavior with different people across different settings and in different contexts, forming a theory along the way. Then they move to quantitative research to test that theory and measure its effects through experimentation and surveys and then make specific statistic-based inferences about the population from representative samples.

Assessing your impact on the life of someone or something should also make use of both methods. Here are some mixed methods to make those evaluations:

- Define what success looks like before beginning.
- Identify if your actions caused others to change their attitudes or behaviors.
- Compare what would have happened without your intervention.
- Look for direct and indirect effects of your impact.
- Identify and measure the type and quantity of evidence.
- See if your impact made it possible for someone to achieve their goals.
- Evaluate the length of impact; does it produce short-term or long-term effects.
- Measure whether it has a net positive or negative effect on well-being; are things getting better or worse.
- Collect anecdotal evidence such as stories and comments.
- Define, monitor, and measure key performance indicators.
- Use appropriate measurement scales for rating or ranking.
- Clearly separate direct causes verses correlations.

> "I've learned that people will forget what you said, people will forget what you did, but people will never forget how you made them feel."
>
> —Maya Angelou

Assignments

🖉 6A: Describe someone who made an impact in your life. How can you measure their influence?

🖉 6B: Describe the impact would you like to make in someone's life right now? Be specific.

🖉 6C: How do you plan to interpret your impact on someone or something with *qualitative* data?

🖉 6D: How do you plan to measure your impact on someone or something with *quantitative* data?

Introduction

Showing initiative and getting out of your rut

How many people do you know that regularly do things without being told? These are the people who are self-starters, who don't hesitate to jump in and get things done. They are resourceful and are able to solve their own problems with very little outside oversight.

Some parents have the fantasy of coming home at the end of a hard day at work and finding that their kids have finished their homework, completed household chores, practiced the piano, and prepared a nutritious and delicious meal for everyone to consume—all on a voluntary basis, without compulsion or an expectation of reward. If such a fantasy was to ever come true—and it might, miracles are real—it can't happen unless your children possess initiative.

If you want others to show more initiative, then you will likely need to lead out and take initiative yourself and show them how it is done.

If you possess the virtue of initiative, you are willing to lead out, make the first move, and take the first step. It is an aggressive readiness combined with the energy to do something that might cause hesitation in others. Taking initiative sets you ahead of your competitors. It gives you visibility and allows you to set the pace. *Carpe diem!*

To acquire this virtue, first, you will learn why it is important to get out of your rut. Have you ever been stuck in a rut where you felt like you were fixed in a predetermined path following the well-worn route blazed and paved by someone else? Do you know the symptoms of stagnation? Do you know how to get unstuck? We'll find out.

Second, work for yourself. Regardless of who signs your paycheck, you are an entrepreneur who works for yourself. You are the master of your own life and the captain of your own ship. Only you can determine how much effort you put into your work—it could be the bare minimum or the maximum amount humanly possible. We'll explore the characteristics you need to successfully be your own boss.

Third, tackle more tasks. If you're trying to make an impression at work or position yourself where you can get a promotion to management, keep in mind that the big jobs usually go to the people who have proven their ability to outgrow the smaller ones. Don't hesitate to tackle tougher jobs and take more risks.

Fourth, seize the day. While it is possible to sit back and wait for opportunities to present themselves before taking them, it is extraordinarily unlikely this will happen. We'll explore the principle of proactivity and how you can make things happen rather than waiting around for your ship to come in.

Fifth, rock the boat. Rocking the boat doesn't necessarily cause bad things to happen. It could, and you should consider the risks before doing it, but it can also initiate meaningful change. Sometimes the hibernating bear needs to be poked—especially if it is blocking your escape from the cave.

Sixth, jump start others. Once you think you start finding regular success in your new groove, you may want to consider sharing what you have learned with others. If it feels right to you, you may want to invite others to follow your example and enhance their lives. Perhaps you can be the spark that jump starts their passion for life and reignites their initiative.

There you have it. These six steps will help you start your own engine and initiate positive changes in your life, giving you the ability to make course corrections and improvements every single day of your life. If you're ready to take action and move forward, then let's get the ball rolling right now. You can do this!

Lesson 1

Get out of your rut

In the United States, before the completion of the transcontinental railroad in 1869, if you wanted to migrate west to build a new life in the wild frontier, you likely traveled by wagon train or stagecoach. If you couldn't afford those options, and wanted to travel a bit faster, you could make your own handcart loaded up with your bare necessities. When it rained, the heavy wagons sank into the muddy trail and created ruts or grooves with their iron wheels. When it dried, and your wagon fell into one of these deep ruts, which could be over two feet deep, you might get "stuck in a rut" and unable to get out and move along. In narrow areas, where you had no choice but to use the trail, these ruts could bring an entire company of pioneers to a slow crawl, if not a dead stop, like an automobile accident on our modern freeways.

Have you ever been stuck in a rut where you felt like you were fixed in a predetermined path following the well-worn route blazed and paved by someone else? Perhaps it is a tradition handed down from one generation to another, such as belonging to a particular religion, celebrating holidays in a particular way, or maintaining certain attitudes or beliefs. Maybe it is your turn to take over the old family business or the family farm even though you'd rather do something different. Perhaps you are stuck in a dead-end job with no hope of advancement. Maybe it is something of your own making, such as a daily routine, a bad habit, or a failing relationship. Maybe you are just tired of doing the same thing over and over again. But for whatever reason, you aren't sure how to get out of it and do something different.

Perhaps you are showing some of these symptoms of stagnation:
- Perceive that every day is like every other day.

- Believe there is nothing else better for you out there.
- Don't see the purpose in anything you do.
- Experience agonizing boredom and monotony.
- Believe your skills are being underutilized or ignored.
- Feel like you're going nowhere no matter how hard you try.
- Can't get worked-up or excited about anything.
- Feel unmotivated, unfulfilled, and uninterested.
- Reminisce about the good old days when things were different.
- Find yourself just trying to endure and survive another day.
- Become easily frustrated or annoyed with colleagues and customers.
- Daydream frequently about doing something else.
- Look at other people's lives with jealousy.

Many people feel like they can't get out of a rut to shake up their routines and habits. In fact, they prefer safe and predictable options rather than doing something that involves risk and a potential for failure. They believe it is far better to be "safe than sorry" and are resigned to a life of inevitable tedium, even though it sucks out their life force and makes them miserable.

Or perhaps they have a difficult time making difficult decisions and prefer that others make them. Maybe they lack the self-discipline to take the more difficult path of initiative rather than taking the lazy, easy road. Some enjoy procrastination and spending time creating alibis and excuses for not getting real work done. Others get paralyzed into inaction by focusing on all the things that might go wrong if they don't do things perfectly. Others have a low self-image and feel they can't do hard things because of past experiences and failures.

Whatever the reason, one thing is certain, they will remain on the turgid treadmill of life as long as they desire. If they choose to have hope in themselves, and learn a handful of skills, they can hop out of the squirrel cage, venture outside, and experience what the wonderful world has to offer. By taking small steps and being open to change, individuals can break free from the monotony of routine and explore new opportunities for growth and happiness.

> "The only difference between a rut and a grave are the dimensions."
>
> —Ellen Glasgow

Assignments

🖉 1A: Do you feel as if you are stuck in a rut in some aspect of your life? Explain.

🖉 1B: What is preventing you from getting out of your rut?

🖉 1C: What are you going to do to get unstuck?

Lesson 2

Work for yourself

Regardless of who signs your paycheck, you are an entrepreneur who works for yourself. It doesn't matter if you're the person at the bottom of the organization chart with seven levels of management above you—you are your own supervisor. When a young child tells their parent, "You aren't the boss of me," they aren't being disrespectful or insubordinate, they are speaking an immanent truth, although a bit prematurely. Once they are of a legal age and have demonstrated the ability to be autonomous and accountable, every individual gets to choose what they think, how they feel, and how they behave. Of course, when making those choices, they also choose the necessary consequences of those thoughts, feelings, and behaviors.

When you choose to work for a company in exchange for a wage or salary, you implicitly agree to obey the company leaders who have purchased the right to direct your work as long as it conforms to mutually acceptable labor standards. But they can't force you to do things you don't want to do. That would be slavery. You must choose to want to do the assigned task, which makes you the ultimate decision-maker. When you choose to stop working, you are also choosing to stop being paid for that work. The buck always stops with you.

As the master of your own life and the captain of your own ship, you determine how much effort you put into your work—it could be the bare minimum or the maximum amount humanly possible. You decide whether to focus your attention on your assignments or let your mind aimlessly wander. You choose how much emotional energy you want to invest in building relationships with your colleagues. Even though you may not be able to control what you work on, you can determine how well you work on it. You can choose to deliver an outstanding performance or sit in the audience and passively watch the action.

> "In a world of bosses, you are your own master."
>
> —John Grogan

As your own boss, not only do you get to call the shots, but you get all the responsibilities that come along with management. You decide whether or not you take ownership and pride in your products or services. You get to figure out how to keep yourself motivated and happy to work hard; fortunately, with an understanding of temperament, you understand exactly what motivates you to capitalize on your strengths and perform at your best. You need to define your goals and create realistic plans to achieve them. You will confidently set schedules and deadlines and unfailingly stick to them. As you passionately perform your work, you will want to look for little improvements, innovations, or shortcuts that can make the process more efficient and productive. You will look for ways to trim the fat and reduce wasted time and energy. As you're juggling all these duties, you will also need to make sure that you keep your personal, family, and social life in balance so you can stay physically, mentally, emotionally, and fiscally healthy—we work to live not live to work.

As you adopt this entrepreneurial mindset and fulfill all these obligations, you always need to keep your customer, which in this case is the person who signs your paycheck, in the forefront of your mind. You want them to be as happy and satisfied as possible. At the end of the day, they should feel as if they got a good return on their investment in you and received more value than they expected to get. If you can regularly provide more benefit than expense, they are far more likely to be a long-term, paying client.

Every individual is ultimately their own boss, responsible for making choices and decisions that will determine their success and satisfaction in their work. By adopting an entrepreneurial mindset, one can take ownership of their work, prioritize goals, and strive for excellence while keeping their customer, in this case, their employer, in mind. With this approach, individuals can not only achieve professional success but also maintain a healthy work-life balance and overall well-being.

Assignments

🖉 2A: What benefits can you receive by adopting an entrepreneurial mindset as you work for others?

🖉 2B: Acting like your own boss often results in becoming a boss sooner than later. How come?

🖉 2C: What characteristics do you need to enhance to successfully be your own boss?

Lesson 3

Tackle more tasks

People who have initiative demonstrate it by taking full responsibility for their life. When things don't work out the way they want them to, rather than sitting back and whining about it, blaming others for their disappointment, or complaining loudly about their circumstances to anyone who will listen, they shift gears. They take the energy that others spent distributing their load of misery to others and spend it to do something that will up their game and enhance their performance. Often, this means that they seek for more responsibilities, take on more challenges, and tackle more tasks.

Sometimes this takes the form of volunteerism, which is the principle of donating something they have, like time, money, or energy, for the benefit of the people they work with or their customers rather than for any financial reward. Perhaps you will take part in or help organize a charity run, a food or gently used clothing drive, or a carnival fund raiser. Maybe you will volunteer and rope others into helping you make or serve food to the homeless. Or maybe you donate blood, unwanted gifts, books, artwork, or organs—although that last one is likely to be a one-off. This isn't completely altruistic or philanthropic in nature because they are hoping it will demonstrate to others that they are willing to go above and beyond the call of duty. If it doesn't do that, that's okay too, because trying to help those who can't help themselves is a good way to counteract the negative effects of emotions like unhappiness, depression, stress, anger, and anxiety. Volunteering makes you happy, increases your self-confidence, and gives you a sense of purpose.

Taking initiative at home, at work, or in your community means that when you spot a problem, rather than hoping that someone will do something about it, you work on it yourself. If you see an obstruction in the road, you pull over and remove it. If you find trash on the trail, you pick it up and pack it out. If you see that the sink is full of dirty dishes, you start doing them and try to get someone to help too. Taking initiative doesn't mean you have to do it all yourself, it means you are going to commit to making sure it gets done, even if you delegate some of the work to others.

> "When you take on more than the norm, your boss can't help but think that you're capable of a bigger role. This includes showing that you're willing to take risks by making innovative suggestions."
>
> —Travis Bradberry

Some people are hesitant to do something because it might be the job of someone else to do it—perhaps someone is being paid to do it. But that rationalization shouldn't stop you in the slightest because it will still make a difference, especially to that person. If it helps you gain a new skill, form friendships, show that you are a team player, and doesn't interfere with your own work, then what's wrong with trying to make the world a better place? If you are worried about overstepping your bounds or making mistakes, take a breather to reassess the situation and make sure your efforts won't cause harm or make someone mad at you. If you can only see positive outcomes and progress, then move forward. No one expects perfection without practice: good jugglers become good throwers and catchers after they have spent weeks dropping tens of thousands of balls.

If you're trying to make an impression at work or position yourself where you can get a promotion to management, keep in mind that the big jobs usually go to the people who have proven their ability to outgrow the smaller ones. Before you take on additional work, make sure you have expertly finished the jobs already assigned to you. If you can do them better or faster than your peer-level colleagues, then you will unquestionably stand out from the rest. This leaves you with some extra time on hand, so use that time to act like a leader by helping your colleagues be as productive as you. This generosity will likely generate gratitude, goodwill, and loyalty from your co-workers—something every manager desires from those they manage. The natural consequence of this is that your new friends may unofficially consider you as their peer leader, which is a step in the right direction. Because you've taken the initiative to help your teammates become more efficient or productive, you have clearly demonstrated leadership qualities. If you continue doing these sorts of things, and can establish a consistent pattern of meaningful leadership, it should be obvious that you are worthy of a promotion. If your company doesn't recognize or reward meritorious behavior like this, then it may not be the right company for you.

Assignments

🖉 3A: How can someone overcome their fear of taking risks and making mistakes?

🖉 3B: Thinking about your current work, what is something you can do to enhance or simplify existing processes or procedures?

🖉 3C: What can you do to take on more responsibilities at work, home, and in the community. Come up with at least three things for all three of those categories.

🖉 3D: How do you deal with colleagues who asks you to take on something that's technically their own responsibility?

Lesson 4

Seize the day

The Latin phrase, *carpe diem,* means that one should seize the day because life is much briefer than we think and we need to live in the moment, regularly stopping to smell the roses throughout the journey. This idea is beautifully expressed in the poem, *To the Virgins, to Make Much of Time,* written in 1648 by Robert Herrick.

Gather ye rosebuds while ye may,
  Old Time is still a-flying;
And this same flower that smiles today
  Tomorrow will be dying.

The glorious lamp of heaven, the sun,
  The higher he's a-getting,
The sooner will his race be run,
  And nearer he's to setting.

That age is best which is the first,
  When youth and blood are warmer;
But being spent, the worse, and worst
  Times still succeed the former.

Then be not coy, but use your time,
  And while ye may, go merry;
For having lost but once your prime,
  You may forever tarry.

While it is possible to sit back and wait for opportunities to present themselves before taking them, it is extraordinarily unlikely this will happen unless you've recently won the lottery and your house is suddenly filled with relatives you've never met and forgotten friends who want you to invest in their crackpot schemes. You don't need to wait for opportunities to knock on your door, you can create them!

This involves the principle of proactivity, where you make things happen that help you achieve your goals rather than reacting to the actions of others. If you don't take the initiative to work on your own dreams, then others will hire you to realize their dreams. A good sport team will not only mount a strong defense to prevent their opponents from scoring, but also launch a robust and dynamic offense; doing only one of those things won't win you the game. Proactive people focus on things they can do, rather than things they can't do. They prefer to act in advance of a future situation so that they can set the pace and take control of the situation.

Viktor Frankl was an Austrian psychiatrist and founder of logotherapy, a form of existential analysis which claimed that finding meaning or purpose in life was the central motivational force in people. He appears to have a largely Blue temperament as is evident in his book, *Man's Search for Meaning* in which he described his experiences in World War II Nazi concentration camps. Even though his freedoms were stripped away, and his body was tortured, he attributed his survival to one freedom that cannot be exterminated: the freedom of thought. He chose to focus on the positive and find meaning and dignity in his existence, inspiring and helping others along the way, including some of his captors. He chose to insert the freedom to choose between the stimulus and response, which allowed him to tap into his self-awareness, imagination, conscience, and independent will to act rather than react. As a result, he turned his life into something extraordinary and inspirational, positively influencing the lives of millions of people.

All too often, people find themselves in unhappy circumstances but are unwilling to take the initiative to change their situation. Perhaps it is because they are conditioned to a life of security, conformity, and preservation and don't want to upset the apple cart. While these things may bring peace of mind, they may also stifle your creativity, muzzle your freedom of expression, and kill off your adventurous spirit. Regardless of your age, your circumstances, or your abilities and disabilities, you have the freedom to choose what your life will be like. While you could yield to your internal moods or be victimized by external conditions, you could also become a dynamic agent of change and create the world you desire.

> "Twenty years from now you will be more disappointed by the things that you didn't do than by the ones you did do. So throw off the bowlines. Sail away from the safe harbor. Catch the trade winds in your sails. Explore. Dream. Discover."
>
> —Mark Twain

Assignments

✏ 4A: What are some things you have always wanted to do or experience but haven't done them yet?

✏ 4B: Why haven't you done those things?

✏ 4C: Pick one of those things and sketch out a plan on how you are going to make it happen.

✏ 4D: What will you do today to seize your day?

Lesson 5

Rock the boat

Stirring the pot, shaking things up, fanning the flame, upsetting the apple cart—these idioms normally convey the notion that you are doing or saying something that upsets people or causes problems. But if you never stirred the pot, wouldn't ingredients burn on the bottom? If you never shook up your salad dressing, wouldn't you get a mouthful of olive oil? If you never fanned the flame, wouldn't it quickly flicker and fizzle out? If you didn't upset the apple cart, wouldn't the apples just sit there and rot?

Rocking the boat doesn't necessarily cause bad things to happen. It could, and you should consider the risks before doing it, but it can also initiate meaningful change. Sometimes the hibernating bear needs to be poked—especially if it is blocking your escape from the cave. If you are interested in initiating change and transforming your world into something that more closely aligns with your dreams, then you must be willing to try something different.

Progress comes when you shift your perspective and creatively think outside of the box. You may need to dismantle something to see how all its components work together so you can improve its design or make it more efficient. You need to be willing to challenge assumptions and experiment with alternatives, otherwise you won't be able to make any improvements. If that means you need to deviate from routines, disrupt patterns, and take risks, then that is what it takes. Your goal isn't to cause harm or damage, but to encourage change and instigate reformations, which might temporarily hurt.

Let's imagine you planted a fruit tree. After planting it, you just can't walk away and let it fend for itself. You will need to regularly check it for pests or disease, protect it from cold spells, and feed it as much fertilizer and water as it needs. If you want the tree to bear high quality fruit, you need to regularly prune back its limbs and thin away some of the unripe fruit so that the tree's energy can be spent improving the size and quality of the remaining crop. If you leave the tree to its natural state, and don't interfere at all, there is a chance the tree may survive on its own, but it certainly won't thrive. At the end of the growing season, you will be lucky to harvest lots of small, unripe, tasteless fruit. If you let it grow wild without maintenance or assistance, eventually the only thing you will be able to harvest is firewood.

If you desire change, but never do anything about it, you are essentially a hypocrite. If you aren't doing everything within your power to bring about necessary change, even if it only within your own life, then your words are just full of hot air. Talk is cheap but making change isn't. It takes an investment of courage, commitment, and dedication. If you can't afford to risk that, then you might as well sit back and enjoy the slow boat ride to nowhere in particular.

Making change requires courage, commitment, and dedication, as well as challenging assumptions, experimenting with alternatives, and thinking creatively outside of the box. However, precautions should also be taken to ensure the safety of yourself and others. Change may not be easy, but it is necessary for growth and improvement.

By the way, if you end up literally rocking the boat, ensure everyone in your boat is wearing a life jacket, otherwise you might end up captive in the clink.

"The hardest thing to remember is that what we each really want is the truth of our lives, good or bad. Not rocking the boat is an illusion that can only be maintained by the unspoken agreement not to feel and in the long run it never really works. Let go of saving the boat and save the passengers instead."

—Kenny Loggins

Assignments

✏ 5A: What are some things in society that need to be altered?

✏ 5B: What are some things in your life that need to be shaken up a bit?

✏ 5C: What will you change, how will you do it, and when will you start?

Lesson 6

Jump start others

Summoning up the conviction to start your own engine and initiate positive changes in your life, and then continuing to make course corrections and improvements every single day, is your most important mission in life. Once you think you've got a handle on it, and are finding routine success in your new groove, you may want to consider sharing what you have learned with others. If it feels right to you, you may want to invite others to follow your example and enhance their lives. Perhaps you can be the spark that jump starts their passion for life and reignites their initiative. Not only will this help them but surrounding yourself with others who are also on a path of self-improvement will help you maintain your resolve whenever you're tempted to revert to bad behaviors.

> "We must make automatic and habitual, as early as possible, as many useful actions as we can... in the acquisition of a new habit, we must take care to launch ourselves with as strong and decided initiative as possible. Never suffer an exception to occur till the new habit is securely rooted in your life."
>
> —William James

Suppose you've made a resolution to lose weight, lift weights, and get in shape. Once you start finding success and are enjoying the fruits of a healthier body, this doesn't mean you have the license to morph into a swankering lunkhead, a perfervid weight-watcher, or a nutritional nagger who goes around foisting their latest passion for health on every passerby. You don't want to become an annoying jerk. You must be much more subtle than that. Setting a positive example, making your lifestyle attractive, and gently inviting people to follow in your footsteps is far more effective than a full-on frontal assault.

Occasionally, it only takes one person to instigate a chain reaction that leads to dramatic change. For instance, in 1955, Rosa Park's brave decision to ignore the Montgomery city bus driver and not surrender her seat to a white person, helped to reinvigorate the United States civil rights movement. Her action inspired the leaders of the local black community to organize a year-long transit boycott led by a young Baptist minister, Dr. Martin Luther King, Jr. Over the next 14 years, hundreds of thousands rallied together in largely peaceful protests until the Civil Rights Act and the Voting Rights Act were passed by Congress.

On June 5, 1989, in Beijing's Tiananmen Square, one day after the Chinese government's violent crackdown on thousands of university students who were demonstrating against the oppressive government, an unidentified young man stood in front of a column of tanks and refused to let them pass. This dramatic event was captured by photographers and videographers and quickly spread around the world, resulting in international pressure on the government to reform and provide more freedoms to its citizens.

As you develop your own initiative, and help others acquire some too, you will find that it provides many benefits, including the motivation and ability to independently assess the need for change and then execute those changes. It gives you the capacity to think creatively and examine the world through a more action-oriented lens. It will transform you from a person who follows the crowd and reacts to changes in their environment, to a person who acts of their own accord to make things happen. It will allow you create plans and programs that will launch you into new spaces, new relationships, and new adventures. The only thing between your dreams and you, is initiative.

Assignments

- 6A: Why does it feel so amazing when you know you are the creator of your reality?

- 6B: What simple action could you take today to produce a new momentum toward success in your life?

- 6C: How does a lack of employee initiative harm the workplace?

- 6D: How can you help the rising generation face challenges and take more initiative?

Introduction

How optimism beats pessimism every single time

Why should we become more optimistic? Here are just a handful of benefits.

Optimism allows us to keep our goals and dreams in sight and in play. It gives us the motivation to keep working on them. It allows us to feel more control over our lives. It encourages us to try again rather than give up. It increases our physical and emotional health. It allows us to experience new or adventurous things. It reduces stress and anxiety. It spurs us on to achieve great things.

Are you ready to acquire more optimism in your life? If so, the future looks really, really bright.

Optimism is the virtue that gives you the tendency to look on the more favorable side of events or conditions and expect the best outcomes. You believe that no matter how bad things look at the moment, things will soon change for the better. You have the ability to rise to any occasion and turn things around to your advantage.

First, let's measure your optimism. We'll see if you need more or already have too much. We'll also figure out which circumstance or roles require more optimism than others. At times it may be advantageous to be highly optimistic, while at other times you need to be somewhere near the realistic middle.

Second, let's learn how to take back control. In this reading assignment we will explore your existing "locus of control" which is a belief about whether the outcomes of your actions are contingent on what you do or on events outside your personal control.

Third, let's discover why it is critical to decrease negativity. Pessimism is much more "sticky" than optimism. Like glue, it is hard to remove once it has touched you. And then you tend to spread it like a viral contagion. We'll figure out how to pay less attention to the bad and give more attention to the good.

Fourth, let's learn how to repeat some aspirational affirmations. An affirmation is a positive statement that we tell ourselves to replace any negative or unhelpful thoughts or feelings that are interfering with our ability to overcome challenges. These aren't mantras, wishful-thoughts, or boastful claims: these are succinct statements about what matters most to us.

Fifth, let's make it a habit to always choose gladness. Is making the choice to see the good a form of delusional self-deception? Not at all. Trying to turn lemons into lemonade is a far more helpful coping strategy than commiserating over the bad. I'll reveal a list of 100 glad behaviors that will help you become more optimistic.

Finally, let's start making some meaningful promises to yourself. Optimists International is an international service club that focuses on spreading optimism. Its members follow the "the Optimist Creed" which is a set of promises you make to yourself that will help you become authentically optimistic. We'll review that creed and try to incorporate it into our lives.

Becoming more optimistic has numerous benefits that can positively impact our lives. It can help us keep our goals in sight and give us the motivation to achieve them. Optimism can also reduce stress and anxiety, increase our physical and emotional health, and encourage us to try again rather than give up. By implementing the six strategies outlined in this reading assignment, we can become more optimistic and experience all the benefits that come with it. Assimilating these six strategies into your life will help you become more optimistic. As a result, you will feel happier, become healthier, have more fun, get more job promotions, bounce back from setbacks, enhance your relationships, and might even live a few years longer. Sounds good to me. Sounds really good!

Lesson 1

Measure your optimism

People often think of optimism and pessimism as opposite sides of the same coin. You are either one or the other and cannot be both at the same time. But it might be more helpful to view optimism as a single continuum, where at one end you have too little optimism (often referred to as pessimism) while on the other end you have too much optimism with unrealistic or improbable expectations, such as spending the winnings from a lottery before your numbers are drawn. Like most things in life, having too little or too much of an attribute can become a liability.

Some circumstances or roles require more optimism than others. At times it may be advantageous to be highly optimistic, while at other times you need to be somewhere near the realistic middle. But it can also be beneficial to be pessimistic in special circumstances, such as trying find motivation to work out contingency plans in case everything really does fall apart. Investing in a little pessimistic insurance may give you the breathing room to enjoy the optimistic dreams of the future.

Below are some characteristics of people who demonstrate high amounts of optimism as well as people with low amounts of optimism (pessimism).

High Optimism	Low Optimism
• Removes roadblocks to their success	• Builds barriers to their success
• Turns the impossible into the possible	• Turns the possible into the impossible
• Changes conditions and circumstances	• Criticizes conditions and circumstances

- Encourages and excites other people
- Expects more good things to happen than bad
- Sees a green near every sand trap
- Celebrates strengths and successes
- Looks at the horizon and sees an opportunity
- Anticipates success
- Believe they have everything they need to succeed
- Wonders how high the kite will fly
- Promotes progress, prosperity, and plenty
- Identifies assets, abundance, and advantages
- Expects the best in uncertain times
- Spreads cheer and approval
- Is excited about future possibilities
- Notices that all doors have handles and hinges
- Predicts parties and celebrations will be enjoyable

- Disparages and discredits other people
- Expects more bad things to happen than good
- Sees a sand trap near every green
- Finds faults and failures
- Peers into the distance and fears a problem
- Anticipates failure
- Believe they lack what they need to succeed
- Wonders how soon the kite will fall
- Preaches limitations, liabilities, and losses
- Identifies mistakes, misfortunes, and misery
- Expects the worst in uncertain times
- Spreads misery and woe
- Is worried about future possibilities
- Notices that doors have locks and latches
- Predicts parties and celebrations will be painful

"One of the things I learned the hard way was that it doesn't pay to get discouraged. Keeping busy and making optimism a way of life can restore your faith in yourself."

—Lucille Ball

Assignments

🖉 1A: Using the lists above, if you had to place yourself on the optimism continuum, where 0 represents no optimism and 10 is complete optimism, where would you sit right now? Where would you prefer to be? Explain.

🖉 1B: What are the pitfalls of being overly optimistic and overly pessimistic?

🖉 1C: Describe some situations where you need to be as optimistic as possible.

🖉 1D: Low optimism can sometimes be beneficial. Identify some applicable scenarios.

Lesson 2

Take back control

If you're like most people, you have learned that in some situations you have absolutely no control over what happens to you. If you have been exposed to a number of these uncontrollable situations, you have also learned to passively hunker down and accept the situation even though it may be uncomfortable, unpleasant, or even painful. You believe it is pointless and unproductive to try to fight back or seek for escape even if an escape route magically appeared in front of you. You accept your state of misery. Because of these past experiences, you are also likely to assume that you have little control in future experiences, and so you expect to perpetually experience a degree of hopelessness, heightened anxiety, and depression whenever you find yourself in similar situations. As a result, you feel used, abused, victimized, and pessimistic about the future.

Sound familiar? Don't worry if it does because scientists tell us this is the normal human response. What is abnormal, however, is to find someone who believes it doesn't have to be that way. Optimists are people who don't believe there is a linear relationship between the past and the future. They believe that smack dab in the middle of this timeline is the present, and that decisions made in the present have the power to affect the future more than decisions in the past. In fact, they actively take steps in the present to build the future they want to see. Psychologists call this an internal locus of control because you believe you control your destiny. Most people with low optimism often have an external locus of control because they believe their fate lies in the hands of others.

Dr. Julian B. Rotter created a locus of control test to determine the extent to which an individual possesses internal or external reinforcement beliefs. Different life circumstances may cause that position to change, which is why it is neither good nor bad to be on one side of the continuum or the other. There are pros and cons to each position. However, the more optimistic you are, the more likely you are to possess an internal locus of control. Let's see where you fit on the control continuum. Below you will see some items from Rotter's test. See if you agree more with the internals or the externals.

Internal Locus of Control

- My misfortunes are the result of mistakes I made.
- In the long run, people get the respect they deserve.
- The idea that leaders are unfair to their followers is nonsense.
- Capable people who fail to become leaders have not taken advantage of their opportunities.
- People who can't get others to like them don't understand how to get along with others.
- Becoming a success is a matter of hard work; luck has little or nothing to do with it.
- The average citizen can have an influence in government decisions.
- When I make plans, I am almost certain that I can make them work.
- In my case, getting what I want has little or nothing to do with luck.
- What happens to me is my own doing.

External Locus of Control

- Many of the unhappy things that happen to me are partly due to bad luck.
- There will always be wars, no matter how hard people try to prevent them.

- Most people don't realize the extent to which their happiness is influenced by accidental happenings.
- Without the right breaks, one cannot be an effective leader.
- No matter how hard you try, some people just don't like you.
- I have often found that what is going to happen will happen.
- You need to be in the right place at the right time to get a good job.
- This world is run by the few people in power, and there is not much the little guy can do about it.
- Many times, we might just as well make decisions by flipping a coin.
- Sometimes I feel that I don't have enough control over the direction my life is taking.

> "A locus of control orientation is a belief about whether the outcomes of our actions are contingent on what we do or on events outside our personal control."
>
> —Philip G. Zimbardo

Assignments

🖉 2A: Describe a time in your life when you had no choice but to obey. How did it make you feel? What lessons did you learn from this experience?

🖉 2B: Describe a time in your life when you had an internal locus of control. What did you learn from that experience?

🖉 2C: When acquiring more optimism, do you think it would help to adopt an internal locus of control? Why or why not?

Lesson 3

Decrease negativity

The question, "Is the glass half-full or half-empty?" quickly sorts people into two groups: optimists or pessimists (and perhaps realists if you think it is both). The optimists view the glass through a positive "gain" frame, while the pessimists view it through a negative "loss" frame. The optimists are looking at what they've gained in the glass, which makes them happy, while the pessimists are thinking about what they lost, which makes them sad. The simple secret of happiness, we are told, is to think like an optimist and look for the positive gains in life.

Unfortunately, social psychologists tell us that pessimism is much more "sticky" than optimism. Like glue, it is hard to remove once it has touched you. It is far more difficult to shift from being negative to positive than vice versa. People tend to get stuck and fixated on the negative, and then they pass it around like a viral contagion. In fact, once you learn something negative about someone or something, you are far more likely to focus on the negative rather than the positive, which is why most elections now-a-days are won through pointing out the weaknesses in an opponent rather than focusing on a candidate's strengths. It takes more mental and emotional energy—more effort—to turn something from a negative into a positive, even if there are an equal number of positive points as negative points. Once the trend goes against you, its momentum keeps it rolling downhill until it reaches the bottom of your personal pit of despair.

So, if you want to be happy, rather than spending the extra effort to replace bad feelings with good feelings, it might be easier to simply set aside the negative from the get-go and focus first on the positive. That doesn't mean you ignore the bad entirely, but you intentionally pay less attention to it and give more attention to the good. If the nay-saying nincompoops on the nightly newscast are making you feel narky and nasty, nix it. If all you do is complain about your day at work when you get home and claim it to be some sort of cathartic release, stop it! Talk about all the good that happened instead. Try to imagine how things can get better. Don't ignore reality but face it while simultaneously trying to put a positive spin on things.

Because of the stickiness of negativity, if you consciously try to spend at least twice as much time on the positives as you do on the negatives, you might be able to break even. The more time you spend on the positives, while restricting the frequency and turning down the intensity of the negatives, the more fulfilled, happier, and productive you will become.

> "Some people see the glass half full. Others see it half empty. I see a glass that's twice as big as it needs to be."
>
> —George Carlin

Assignments

- 3A: What are the sources of negativity in your life? Which can be eliminated? Which can be reduced in frequency or intensity?

- 3B: Make a list of the things you have today that you wouldn't have had 100 years ago.

- 3C: Rather than dwelling on negative statistics, what are some positive statistics that we see in today's world? Look for things where the trend is going in a much more favorable direction. For example, illiteracy is going down. What else?

- 3D: Write down three things you're looking forward to. Let the good feelings sink in for at least five minutes.

- 3E: Listen to songs or look at photos from your past that stir up positive memories and feelings of nostalgia. How does this boost your optimism?

Lesson 4

Repeat aspirational affirmations

An affirmation is a positive statement that we tell ourselves to replace any negative or unhelpful thoughts or feelings that are interfering with our ability to overcome challenges. Unlike a mantra that is repeatedly chanted to gain spiritual insight, an affirmation is a simple phrase that we periodically repeat to ourselves throughout the day which highlights a characteristic or quality that we admire or desire to obtain. An affirmation isn't wishful-thinking or boastful claims: it succinctly codifies our values and describes what matters most to us. It brings our aspirations back into focus whenever we lose sight of our goals.

> "You've been criticizing yourself for years and it hasn't worked. Try approving of yourself and see what happens."
>
> —Louise Hay

Positive self-talk has been researched by psychologists and neuroscientists because they seem to make a big difference in the lives of millions of people. Celebrities like Jim Carrey, Denzel Washington, Jennifer Lopez, and Oprah Winfrey swear to the effectiveness of affirmations. Evidence suggests it helps to lower stress, improve academic achievement, enhance self-worth, ease anxiety, enhance performance, and lower depression. When faced with something that threatens your personal identity or sense of well-being, repeating an affirmation helps you remember the strengths, qualities, and attributes that you admire or may already possess. It allows you to get your mind back on your immediate goals.

You might choose to gather a handful of simple affirmations that you can commit to memory. Or you may want to post them on your bathroom mirror, a refrigerator door, or on your dashboard. You can silkscreen them onto t-shirts, emboss them on coffee cups, or, if you're really committed, tattoo them to your body. Stick them someplace where you are likely to notice them throughout the day. Then, whenever you see it, you read it aloud. Or, when you start to encounter some unproductive negative feelings or thoughts, stop what you are doing and immediately recall or repeat your positive statements.

Affirmations should be tied to aspects of our current character or things that we value most in life. They could also be quotes, phrases, proverbs, scriptures, song lyrics, slogans, or one-liners that you find particularly inspirational. As we know, each personality type has a set of strengths and characteristics that they are likely to possess. This would be a great place to start when building your own collection. Below are some example affirmations that reflect the values of each of the four temperaments. Once you figure out how to do your own primary color well, use these affirmations to help you adopt the attitudes and behaviors of the other colors in your spectrum.

Blue

- I am great with people.
- People like me because I care.
- Feelings are important too.
- Families are forever.
- I am grateful for the good things in my life.
- Love one another.
- I will live happily ever after.

- I surround myself with positive people.
- I am an original masterpiece.
- I am beautiful inside and out.
- I am fiercely loyal and beautifully vulnerable.
- I love with my whole heart and soul.
- I am kind and compassionate.
- I am the world's greatest hugger.
- Hate cannot drive out hate; only love can do that.
- My religion is kindness.
- I am my own best friend.
- I am a rainbow in someone's cloud.
- A warm smile is the universal language of kindness.
- Wherever you go, go with all your heart.
- My family and friends are my strength and refuge.
- I am a peacemaker who promotes nonviolent responses.

Gold

- I can be soft in my heart and firm in my boundaries.
- I know what is right and what is wrong.
- I am a responsible and reliable person.
- Hard work is the key to success.
- Obedience is better than sacrifice.
- Cleanliness is next to godliness.
- Life is accepting what is and working from that.
- I will persist when others quit.
- I am worthy of a great life.
- The world needs my contributions.
- There is no substitute for hard work.
- Preparation is the key to success.

- Whatever thou art, act well thy part.
- I enjoy living in a clear and uncluttered space.
- Every day and in every way I am becoming more honorable.
- I have the power to reach my goals.
- I will not procrastinate—the time will never be just right.
- I am the most reliable and stable person around.
- I show my love by what I do for others.
- I reap what I sow.
- Practice makes perfect.
- I am responsible for myself, and I start there.

Green

- Life is a question and how we live it is our answer.
- All problems have solutions.
- I only compare myself to myself.
- I am calm, cool, and collected.
- I can learn anything with enough time and space.
- My head rules my heart.
- I thrive on mental challenges.
- Live long and prosper / make it so.
- Is that your final answer?
- A mind is like a parachute; it doesn't work if it is not open.
- All great achievements require time.
- Don't find fault, find a remedy.
- To improve is to change; to be perfect is to change often.
- I am the architect of my fate.
- I trust my abilities and am stronger than I look.
- I do not need people's approval of my work.
- I am getting smarter every day.

- I will solve the mysteries of life.
- I am still learning so it's okay to make mistakes.
- I seek out mystery in the ordinary.
- I tell the truth about who I am and what I need from others.
- I will allow myself to evolve.

Orange

- Carpe diem: seize the day.
- I can get through anything.
- I am free to make my own choices.
- Live like there's no tomorrow.
- Laugh like today is all you've got.
- Shine like the whole universe is yours.
- Today is a fresh start.
- Life is an adventure and getting wherever you are going is half the fun.
- It's better to be a lion for a day than a sheep all your life.
- Run when you can, walk if you have to, crawl if you must—just never give up.
- No one remembers who came in second.
- I am able to exceed under pressure.
- I am full of vitality and courage.
- My positive attitude is my biggest asset.
- I will strike while the iron is hot.
- I will stop and smell the roses.
- I love to be surrounded by cheerful people.
- I want to discover my limits.
- I am okay with my imperfections.
- I was born to conquer and shine.

- I will not be all talk; I will actually do something!
- Actions speak louder than words.
- I am in charge of how I feel, and I choose to feel happy.
- I embrace change seamlessly and rise to the new opportunity it presents.
- I have come farther than I would have ever thought possible.
- I have everything I need to succeed.

Assignments

🖉 4A: Create 10 affirmational statements that would help anyone, regardless of their personality type, feel more optimistic.

🖉 4B: Identify three affirmations that you will repeat 3 to 5 times every day this week.

Lesson 5

Choose gladness

Pollyanna is a 1913 novel by Eleanor Porter which describes the attitudes and behaviors of an optimistic orphan who tries to find something to be glad about in every situation. As she interacts with the people in her neighborhood, her positivity begins to spread and makes a dramatic difference in the lives of its residents.

Critics of the story point out that someone who is excessively optimistic is dangerously blind to reality and is practicing self-deception and wishful thinking. But are they? Isn't trying to find the good in life and turning lemons into lemonade a more helpful coping strategy than commiserating over the bad?

> "Once you replace negative thoughts with positive ones, you'll start having positive results."
>
> —Willie Nelson

You see, optimists aren't naive idealists who dwell in fantasy lands. They don't ignore the world's bad events, conditions, and people. They face reality head-on and accept its imperfections, letdowns, and limitations. They accept and love the world as it was, is, and will be and do not focus on what was not, is not, or cannot be. They choose to react in positive, constructive ways that enhance their lives and the lives of those around them. They simply choose to be glad. Below are 100 optimistic behaviors that are likely to make you feel gladder.

Glad Behaviors

- Do at least one thing you enjoy each day.
- Crank up your favorite tunes.
- Pick up some trash in your neighborhood.
- Retreat to your happy place.
- Periodically do challenging and meaningful things.
- Express your emotions in healthy ways.
- Find a mentor who can help you do something.
- Work with a therapist if you need more support.
- Forget about past—focus on the future.
- Don't make "to do" lists—make "I just did" lists.
- Take breaks from social media.
- Go outside and get some fresh air.
- Spend money on experiences, not just things you need.
- Work on improving a weakness.
- Read something that isn't serious.
- Play with a puppy or kitten.
- Volunteer to do some charity work and serve others.
- Don't try to predict the future.
- Say thank-you to everyone you meet.
- Do something that engages all your senses.
- Repeat some positive affirmations to help you focus.
- Take a 10 minute meditation break.
- Live according to your personal values.
- Don't blame or shame others.
- Connect with others in your community.
- Explore other cultures and customs.
- Post a positive message for someone to see.

- Break out of your routines and mix things up.
- Do something kind for someone else.
- Don't even think about flipping birdies.
- Embrace the diversity that surrounds you.
- Don't get sucked into negative conversations.
- Walk out your frustrations.
- Get sweaty at least three times a week.
- See yourself as a cause, not an effect.
- Learn something new or interesting.
- Do just one thing at a time.
- Work on your favorite hobby.
- Surround yourself with supportive, positive people.
- Think about what your life would be like with the positives.
- Focus on your success and proven strengths.
- Listen to your inner-voice or conscience.
- Seek out meaningful conversations.
- Express gratitude for the simplest things.
- Incorporate stress relievers into your day.
- Don't worry about what others think.
- Forgive others and let go of the past.
- Look at memes, vids, pics, or posts that make you giggle.
- Make positive memories.
- Smile and flash your pearly whites.
- Learn from your emotions.
- Eliminate all negative self-talk.
- Boost your health with something nutritious and delicious.
- Hold the door open for someone.
- Find your purpose in life.

- Clear the clutter off your counters.
- Wear something that makes a bold statement.
- Give up trying to be superior to anyone.
- Have meaningful, non-trivial conversations.
- Give yourself a little luxurious treat.
- Look for silver linings when facing challenges.
- Stop comparing yourself to others.
- Plan to do something fun and pleasurable.
- Start small—don't attempt to take on everything at once.
- Fake it until you make it.
- Spend some time in nature.
- Turn off your auto-pilot and live in the moment.
- Ditch your phone for at least an hour every day.
- Stop whining and complaining.
- Challenge any negative thoughts.
- Write down three positive things immediately.
- Create or imagine something wonderful.
- Identify a positive role model.
- Limit mood-altering substances, such as drugs or alcohol.
- Join a club or team that reflects your interests.
- Spend a little money on someone else.
- Look for solutions to everyday problems.
- Do something where time just flies by.
- Speak up and be yourself.
- Don't set unrealistic expectations.
- Text "You're awesome" to a friend.
- Send out a thoughtful email to an old friend.
- Find something to look forward to.

- Place an attractive flower or picture in your room.
- Attribute positive results to your abilities.
- Attribute negative results to your lack of effort.
- Silence your obnoxious inner critic.
- Keep a journal of "happy thoughts."
- Imagine yourself in successful scenarios.
- Keep moving forward towards your goals, no matter what.
- Transform challenges into exciting adventures.
- Add your creative and distinctive touch to things.
- Schedule time to unwind, relax, and recoup.
- Do activities that you are already good at doing.
- Avoid media that brings out your worst attributes.
- Play with a child (with the permission of their parent.)
- Issue meaningful compliments to others.
- Do nice things for others, even if you don't feel like it.
- Steer conversations away from yourself and towards others.
- Remember you're not alone—reach out when you need help.

Assignments

🖉 5A: List 5 things that make you feel like your life is good in some way today.

🖉 5B: Think about a time when something did not go as expected or caused you pain and frustration. Briefly write down what that situation was. Look for 3 things about that situation that may help you see the "silver lining."

Lesson 6

Make promises to yourself

As you adopt the characteristics of an optimist, imagine you are on the world's greatest roller coaster ride. Obviously, you are going to encounter lots of ups and downs because if you didn't have the ups, you wouldn't have the downs. After you ascend your way to the top of the lift hill, you immediately start screaming as you drop down from the crest and experience dives, airtime, barrel rolls, bank turns, camelbacks, cobra rolls, helixes, inversions, g-forces, and loops. You should expect lots of shrieks, some fear, a little bit of panic, some queasiness, and a whole lot of fun. It will certainly be a memorable experience, one way or another.

> "The only limits to the possibilities in your life tomorrow are the buts you use today."
>
> —Les Brown

Life is a whole lot like that roller coaster because you will often find yourself hopelessly strapped in where all you can do it hold tight and wait for the experience to end. Whether you walk away from it laughing, sobbing, or puking your guts out—that decision is entirely up to you. You have the freedom to choose to act in positive ways rather than being acted upon. You decide the person you'll be. You can choose to be an optimistic or a pessimist, you decide whether you want an internal or external locus-of-control, you control whether you fill your life with positivity or negativity. Stop being your own worst enemy and start becoming your own best advocate. Take the time to learn how to trade your negative thoughts and unproductive worries for the positive attitudes and constructive actions that will help you find more joy in life.

As you adopt the attitudes and behaviors of an optimist, frequently consider the composition below. It is marvelously aspirational in nature and can help you stay focused on your goals. It was written in 1912 by Christian D. Larson, one of early advocates of unlocking the power of your mind to find more success in life. A version of it was later called "The Optimist Creed" and has become the manifesto of Optimist International, an international service club with thousands of units around the world.

Promise Yourself

- To be so strong that nothing can disturb your peace of mind.
- To talk health, happiness, and prosperity to every person you meet.
- To make all your friends feel that there is something worthwhile in them.
- To look at the sunny side of everything and make your optimism come true.
- To think only of the best, to work only for the best and to expect only the best.
- To be just as enthusiastic about the success of others as you are about your own.
- To forget the mistakes of the past and press on to the greater achievements of the future.
- To wear a cheerful expression at all times and give a smile to every living creature you meet.
- To give so much time to improving yourself that you have no time to criticize others.

- To be too large for worry, too noble for anger, too strong for fear, and too happy to permit the presence of trouble.
- To think well of yourself and to proclaim this fact to the world, not in loud word, but in great deeds.
- To live in the faith that the whole world is on your side, so long as you are true to the best that is in you.

Assignments

🖉 6A: Make four different lists containing (1) things you worry about, (2) things that are causing you anger, (3) things that you fear, and (4) things that are causing trouble in your life.

🖉 6B: What are some supportive responses you can give to people who are currently feeling victimized and hopeless?

🖉 6C: As you develop more optimism, you will want to associate with positive people who are willing to encourage and support you, while steering clear of negative people who criticize or doubt. Make a list of the positive people in your life who can help you be more optimistic.

Introduction

Stepping up your performance to achieve success

Do you consider yourself to be a performer? That doesn't necessarily mean you find yourself up on a stage or in the spotlight, but that, through either talent, luck, or hard work, you can do something so well that it becomes wonderful to watch. I bet there is something that you can do that is inspiring to others. You just need to uncover it and work on it until it is ready to be seen by others. We all have natural talents, hidden strengths, different gifts, and the capacity to achieve more than we think is possible.

Finding personal satisfaction, bringing other people joy, adding light to a darkening world—all of these things are the result of someone turning in a good performance. Let's figure out how to perform at our best, even if your best is only seen by you.

Possessing the virtue of performance, you are a natural performer and have the inherent ability to excel in any of the arts, from the fine arts to the performing arts to the industrial arts. You are entertaining, charming, and humorous and tend to liven up the room with your presence. You would rather be an active player than a passive spectator.

Like it or not, we are all actors standing on the stage of life. We all have a role to perform, and most of us have many roles to perform, some at the exact same time. Learning to perform these roles to the best of our ability and become an inspirational performer, is an awesome goal. It is a virtuous goal. So here are the six performance enhancing steps we'll study that will help you step up your success.

First, narrow your focus. One of the keys to success is not to focus on too many things at the same time and become spread too thin. Focus on doing one thing so well that it becomes instinctive or almost automatic.

Second, passionately deliver value. Being in love with the work you do and being passionate about it is very important and makes it much easier to work for extended periods of time. But it also needs to be coupled with a sense of purpose or mission. We'll learn how to combine passion with purpose.

Third, prime your pump. This is where we warm up our minds and bodies and get our juices flowing so that we can work with momentum. We'll discover how our mood affects our performance.

Fourth, upgrade your thoughts. Just like we upgrade our computers from time-to-time, we also need to upgrade our brains. If we want to enhance our focus or increase our performance and productivity, that means we need to change how we think since our thoughts direct our behaviors.

Fifth, make micro adjustments. I'll reveal a number of popular and effective ways to make slow, incremental improvements to your performance. We'll work on creating and prioritizing our own top 10 lists of micro adjustments.

Sixth, enjoy the flow. The phenomenon called "flow" occurs when your performance has reached its optimum level. This state occurs about 10 to 20 percent of the time for those at the top of their game. Everything is going your way and you feel "in the zone." We'll also learn about the companion state of "clutch" and when we need to employ it.

Achieving a truly remarkable and brilliant performance takes a fair amount of effort, but it is within anyone's grasp. The only limits you'll encounter are the limits you place on yourself or the limits you have allowed others to place on you. Let's finally shed those shackles once and for all. Please join me as we step up our performance and acquire this praiseworthy virtue.

Lesson 1

Narrow your focus

Psychiatrists and psychologists use the 947-page *Diagnostic and Statistical Manual of Mental Disorders* to determine which mental disorder someone may be experiencing. *Obsession* is a disorder which is defined as "recurrent and persistent thoughts, urges, or images that are experienced, at some time during the disturbance as intrusive and inappropriate, and that cause marked anxiety and distress." If thoughts and urges are unwanted, or cause stress and anxiety, then it is a bad thing. But if they are wanted, or even sought out, and produce favorable results, then it becomes one of the biggest assets of top performers. We usually call this positive behavior "focus" or "passion" rather than the more negative "obsession," but it simply means that you can center your attention on something so intensely that it becomes a valuable skill or process in your life.

One of the keys to success is not to focus on too many things at the same time. Multitasking is a myth. You will spend more time and cognitive energy trying to work on multiple concurrent tasks then you would if you just focused on one task at a time. Unless you have more than one brain, like computers that have more than one microprocessor, you won't be able to do things simultaneously—they may appear to be simultaneous, but in reality, a switch is being made superfast that makes the sequential look like it is working in parallel. Every time that switch is thrown, it takes up energy, slows things down, causes anxiety, creates mistakes, inhibits creativity, increases complexity, and makes you less productive overall.

If you want to enhance your performance, focus on doing one thing so well that it becomes instinctive or almost automatic. Become so fascinated and enthralled in refining it that you appear to be obsessed with it. This means you aren't satisfied with your existing behaviors or performances, but that you are intentionally making today's repetition incrementally better than yesterday's effort. This means you must be on the constant lookout for the tiniest of mistakes or trying out new hacks or procedures that produce small improvements.

People who regularly perform below expectations are often spread too thin. Even if they bumped-up their efforts to 50 or 60 hours per week, they get less done then those who focused for 40 hours on completing one task at a time. Often, pressures to do more come from misguided bosses who establish too many goals, priorities, metrics, tasks, reports, or assign too many workers to collaborate when collaboration may not be needed. But sometimes, to catch the attention or praise of a supervisor, you volunteer to do more even though you are already barely keeping your head above water. It might be far better to dial it back and focus on a couple of tasks until you become the best worker to perform those tasks, rather than the team member who creates a spectacle by juggling too many balls. Obsess to be the best, or better than the rest, before moving on to your next quest.

> "It is vain to do with more what can be done with less."
>
> —William of Ockham

Assignments

✎ 1A: What are some obstacles that get thrown in your way that prevent you from focusing on one task at a time? What can you do to go around or remove those obstacles?

✎ 1B: What is something you already do that is better than most?

✎ 1C: What would you like to do better than others?

Lesson 2

Passionately deliver value

Being in love with the work you do and being passionate about it is very important and makes it much easier to work for extended periods of time. The more personally satisfying it is, the more you enjoy it, the more likely you are to continue doing it with your heart, mind, and strength. But passion by itself doesn't predict success. There are millions of unemployed or underemployed workers who let their passion dictate what they did in the workplace, only to find out that it didn't necessarily pay the bills—just ask an actor in Hollywood or a musician in Nashville. Highly passionate people may start innovative ventures, but 9 out of 10 of these startups will pack it in within a decade. Passion is an important ingredient in any endeavor, to be sure, but it also needs to be coupled with a sense of purpose or mission.

Purpose is the notion that you are providing something of value to the world. It either makes someone's life better or easier, or it makes some aspect of the world more wonderful than it would have been without it. Whether it takes the form of a product or service, others must recognize its importance and make the decision to give you their money in exchange for it. The more genuine, intrinsic value they get from it, the more they are willing to pay. If your performance is valuable to you, but not to them, you better turn it into a money-sucking hobby rather than a money-making vocation.

When you combine passion with purpose, you've got yourself a sensational strategy. Every goal, every task, every enhancement you make to your performance must always have the end consumer in mind. Fixing a problem in the assembly process is good because it speeds up production. Shortening delivery times is good because it benefits the customer. Adding a feature that customers have requested is perfect, even if it means you need to raise prices, because once people know you have their best interests at heart, they will trust you and pay what you ask.

Sometimes, this passion and purpose combine to help you come up with something that is new or innovative that the world hasn't seen before. The more unique it is, the less competition you have, the more value it provides, the more people will demand it from you. Expect to see competitors jealous about your success and attempt to come in and produce knockoffs, but meanwhile, keep that passion and purpose alive to further improve or innovate. Use this energy to drive you to go the extra mile and make each hour you work far more productive, meaningful, and rewarding than those who don't have passion and purpose.

> "You don't get paid for the hour. You get paid for the value you bring to the hour."
>
> —Jim Rohn

Assignments

- 2A: Thinking about your preferences and abilities, where can you get a job that taps into your passion and provides a purpose?

- 2B: How can you get more passionate or find a meaningful purpose in a career you already have?

- 2C: Who do you know that has combined passion and purpose to find success and fulfillment in their work?

- 2D: How can you expand the role of creativity or innovation in your current job?

- 2E: What can you do to make sure you are providing something that is highly valued by others?

Lesson 3

Prime your pump

In rural areas outside of the reach of a municipal water distribution network, you may need to use a pump to draw water from a well. If your pump has not been electrified, you may need to use a mechanical pitcher pump powered purely by your arm muscles. Sometimes, air gets into the pipeline or in the pump itself, and regardless of how vigorously you work the pump, it won't suction up the water. To solve the problem, you pour some water into the top of the pump to displace the air and form a vacuum seal. Then once the pump is primed, it works just fine. If you are roaming the countryside and feel thirsty, and you see a hand pump with a bucket of water sitting next to it, don't drink that water—use it to prime the pump so you can get as much water as you need.

Regardless of whether your performance takes place sitting in front of a canvas, camera, crowd, or computer, you also need to prime your pump before beginning. If you've attended an instrumental concert, you'll hear the musicians warming up and tuning up before the concert begins. If you've been backstage at a play, before the actors set foot on stage, they go through a warm-up ritual. Runners, before the race begins, will stretch and loosen their joints, and warm-up their muscles. Without a proper 5 to 10-minute warm-up, and the increased muscle temperature and blood flow it provides, they might even suffer an injury. Human bodies don't respond very well with sudden changes from dormancy to activity. Abrupt or extreme shifts in state release a variety of chemicals and hormones into our systems that often feel like panic, stress, and anxiety. These reactions don't occur if you take a few minutes to warn your body that difficult tasks are about to occur. By taking the time to warm-up physically you are more likely to turn in a better performance.

Warming up is also good for your emotional well-being. If you've ever tried to do something when you were in a foul mood, you know all about this phenomenon. Even though you possess the physical skills to do something, your head is off brooding in a distant corner. Negative emotions and bad attitude always hurt your performance. To remedy this, you need to do something that will enhance your emotions and put you into a good mood. While physically warming up, some people pray for divine assistance, some recite positive "I can do this" affirmations, some look at pictures of their family for inspiration, while others tell jokes or look at funny videos. You need to create a physical and mental routine that works for you. In fact, once you find a routine that regularly leads to success, keep on repeating it before each performance. It will psychologically condition you to have success even on those days when you don't feel like performing.

"The common conception is that motivation leads to action, but the reverse is true—action precedes motivation. You have to prime the pump and get the juice flowing, which motivates you to work on your goals. Getting momentum going is the most difficult part of the job, and often taking the first step is enough to prompt you to make the best of your day."

—Robert J. McKain

Assignments

✎ 3A: Besides warming-up your body and enhancing your emotions, you can also warm-up your brain. What might that look like?

✎ 3B: Have you ever witnessed or experienced a poor performance because of a foul mood? Explain.

✎ 3C: What is your plan to prime your pump both mentally and physically?

Lesson 4

Upgrade your thoughts

Just like we upgrade our computers from time-to-time, we also need to upgrade our brains. Our brain, just like every other part of our body, benefits from proper nutrition to keep glucose levels steady, regular exercise for increased blood flow to the brain, and sufficient sleep. Sometime our brains might be deficient in certain chemicals which make us susceptible to mental disorders, but those too can be counteracted with appropriate pharmaceuticals. Of course, there are also plenty of legal and illegal substances that harm our brains and affect our ability to make good judgments, and these should be avoided like we avoid contracting computer viruses and malware that affect the performance, integrity, or security of our computers. Healthy bodies usually produce healthy brains.

But a healthy brain is simply the hardware. We also need to upgrade our software. That is how we use our brains. For instance, if we want to enhance our focus or increase our performance and productivity, that means we need to change how we think since our thoughts direct many of our behaviors. We need to spend some time learning how to enhance our mental abilities, such as learning how to study more efficiently, attempting to solve challenging puzzles or problems, trying to memorize things, logically analyzing what we read or hear, learning how to tune-out distractions and focus our attention, learning how to visualize and set realistic life goals, and so on. If we want a healthy brain, we can't sit back and let our brains atrophy and become intellectually lazy. Mental exercise is every bit as important as physical exercise.

For example, every day we choose what we will focus on. If we want to feel discouraged or depressed, we will focus on our past failures, problematic relationships, and our history of poor performance. On the other hand, we could shift our focus from the negative to the positive and focus our brain's energy on the parts of our life can create joy, passion, and fulfillment. We can choose to focus on the values, attitudes, and behaviors that allow us to act in ways that enhance our lives and the lives of those around us. When we make positive choices and intentionally do the things that matter most, we have far more clarity. That clarity allows us to invest our mental energy into achieving desirable goals and becoming a proactive person rather than a reactive person.

Another way we can exercise our brains is take advantage of its native neuroplasticity—its ability to form new brain cells and form neural connections. This process is used whenever we learn something new, change our assumptions, adopt new attitudes, or acquire new habits. This is known as *structural* plasticity where the brain changes its physical structure as a result of learning. In fact, the amount of neuroplasticity expands as we do new things, and contracts when we don't. It is what allows us to adapt to our changing world, enhance our performance, and increase our productivity. It is why psychologists try to teach you new ways of thinking and acting to overcome mental disorders or why athletic coaches encourage you to improve your performance slowly and incrementally. Furthermore, if we experience some sort of brain injury or have killed off some of our brain cells through substance abuse, neuroplasticity allows our brains to move its functions from a damaged area to an undamaged area—scientists call this *functional* plasticity. If we want to remain competent and coherent as we age, and not suffer through some of the mental degradation that naturally occurs with age, we should do all we can to maintain or expand both the structural and functional neuroplasticity of our brains.

> "As human, we all have the same human potential, unless there is some sort of retarded brain function. The wonderful human brain is the source of our strength and the source of our future, provided we utilize it in the right direction. If we use the brilliant human mind in the wrong way, it is really a disaster."
>
> —Dalai Lama

Assignments

✏ 4A: What thoughts or mindsets tend to hold you back?

✏ 4B: If you had to deliver a strong performance at work, and you're experiencing stress or self-doubt, what are some positive phrases that will reduce your anxiety?

✏ 4C: Research shows that optimistic expectations are a reliable predictor of achievement. Why do you think the words you allow yourself to believe significantly impact your outcomes?

Lesson 5

Make micro adjustments

What About Bob? is a comical 1991 movie that features the relationship between an obsessive-compulsive neurotic, Bob Wiley, and his psychotherapist, Dr. Leo Marvin. In the movie, Dr. Marvin has written a book called, *Baby Steps: A Guide to Living Life One Step at a Time* which suggests that to overcome a big challenge, you need to break it down into little challenges. To help do that, you first need to "take a vacation from your problems," which in this case, motivated Bob to insinuate himself into Dr. Martin's family while they were vacationing in their lake-front home.

> "Practice the philosophy of continuous improvement. Get a little bit better every single day."
>
> —Brian Tracy

The idea of taking baby steps towards tackling bigger problems, as well as the notion of taking a vacation from your problems, are both genuine techniques commonly used by psychologists to help their patients overcome their challenges. If we set aside the pain we feel from our past imperfections or failures, and instead, turn our attention towards taking small, incremental steps towards improving our thoughts and actions, our performance will necessarily improve. If we try to tackle too much too soon, which often happens in our self-improvement efforts, we set ourselves up for quick failure. We need to be much more realistic and reach for slow and sustained enhancements rather than an overnight transformation. Running faster than you have strength is a recipe for exhaustion before you finish the race.

Below is a list of some of the most popular ways to make slow, incremental improvements to your performance. Choose one and work on it every day. Once you've mastered it, go back, and choose another. These are very general suggestions that are provided as an aid to help you develop your own individualized and highly specific goals.

- Don't be apathetic or do things half-heartedly.
- Focus on what you do have rather than on what you don't have yet.
- Face the truth and fix your mistakes as soon as possible.
- Sketch out each day with the most important things taking top priority.
- Limit the time you spend with distractions.
- Find someone to help you stay motivated to improve.
- Learn something new every day that will enhance your performance.
- Be patient with yourself but never allow yourself to give up or give in.
- Take personal responsibility for your own performance—never blame others.
- Keep your focus on the present task at hand.
- Maintain positive attitudes and thoughts about your potential.
- Regularly take time to enjoy nature and the wonders of this world.
- Focus on one thing at a time—no multi-tasking.
- Cope with disappointments in constructive ways.
- Help others who are also trying to succeed.

- Abandon thoughts of perfection; just try to get better today than you were yesterday.
- Be multidimensional; don't too lopsided as you live your life.
- Practice so often that your behavior requires little thought.
- Believe that your personal trajectory is only limited by your willingness to move in a different direction.
- Don't be afraid to explore the usual and unusual as you look for improvement.
- Work on improving your speed, consistency, and accuracy.
- Mediate and focus your thoughts and energy for at least 5 to 10 minutes every day.
- Avoid habits and behaviors that harm yourself or others.
- Courageously take bold steps to overcome your weaknesses and do what needs to be done.
- Keep your mind and body as healthy as possible.
- Allow the stress of competition to improve your performance.
- Be attentive to the little details.
- Before performing, visualize yourself doing the activity successfully.

Assignments

- 5A: Think of a metaphor that you can associate with successful and less successful performances.

- 5B: In your experience, what are the primary psychological characteristics that distinguish between more and less successful performances?

- 5C: How does competition help you become a better performer?

- 5D: Make a list of the top 10 micro adjustments you would like to make to your performance. Then sort those from most important to least important.

Lesson 6

Enjoy the flow

How do you know when you are at your peak performance? According to psychologists, the phenomenon called "flow" occurs when your performance has reached its optimum level. This state occurs about 10 to 20 percent of the time for those at the top of their game. Everything is going your way and you feel "in the zone." During this state, you are so caught up in the moment that it doesn't seem to take any attention or effort to perform. Your body appears to be running on autopilot and your body parts are working exactly as intended. Your thoughts are positive, with no negative or critical attitudes, in fact, you might even lose your self-consciousness. Your emotions are under control even though all your senses are fully aroused. You are so engrossed in the activity that time and space seem to stand still.

> "Flow is being completely involved in an activity for its own sake. The ego falls away. Every action, movement, and thought follows inevitably from the previous one, like playing jazz. Your whole being is involved, and you're using your skills to the utmost."
>
> —Mihaly Csikszentmihalyi

Flow is often triggered during your performance as you experience something new or are uncertain as to what is going to happen next. Your mind is not on your performance but is just taking in and enjoying the experience. Some people enter the flow state when things are going so well that they push out their boundaries and explore or experiment with different techniques because they are confident everything will work out okay regardless of what they do. If you are in flow you feel on top of the world, knowing that you are giving your best effort. At the conclusion of the performance, even if you don't win the competition, you are often energized, gratified, and ready to do it all over again because the activity is intrinsically rewarding.

But the transcendent flow state isn't as common as we would like it to be. It can be relatively hard to reach. A much more common psychological state is called "clutch." This occurs when you are faced with important moments or when the outcome is on the line, and you feel pressured to step up and do something truly outstanding. It occurs when you realize that if you pull out all the stops, and give it everything you got, you might deliver the winning performance. Clutch is a more conscious state than flow because your mind is completely and deliberately focused on achieving a fixed goal, such as passing the next person in the race. You decided to make an intense and focused effort to succeed. Because you have a heightened awareness about exactly what needs to be done, you can work through your immediate pain and discomfort to do it. However, unlike flow, at the end of a climactic clutch state, you often feel exhausted and need time to recover and recharge.

In order to reach your peak performance, it's important to understand the concept of "flow" and "clutch." While flow occurs when everything is going smoothly and you are in the zone, clutch is when you consciously focus on achieving a specific goal, such as passing the person in front of you in a race. Both of these states can lead to powerful feelings of motivation, confidence, and enjoyment, and are available to anyone who wants to improve their performance. So, keep striving to do your best, and who knows, you might just experience the nirvana of flow or the intensity of clutch in your next performance.

The nice thing is that both the flow and clutch states share some positive elements in common. Despite the nirvana of flow or the intense pressure of clutch, you genuinely enjoy what you are doing, feel extra motivation to perform at your best, perceive you are in complete control of your actions, become entirely absorbed in the performance, and have all the confidence you need. Fortunately, these powerful feelings are available to anyone who wants to deliver a stellar performance. If you haven't yet experienced these effects, then you perhaps you still have some room to improve. Just remember, peak performance doesn't necessarily mean winning performance—you may not be the top artist, athlete, author, or artisan—but you are doing as best as you can right now. You might do even better tomorrow.

Assignments

- 6A: Have you experienced a state of flow? If so, explain how it felt.

- 6B: Have you experienced a state of clutch? If so, explain how it felt.

- 6C: Why is feedback on your performance important?

- 6D: What are some barriers to achieving flow in the workplace?

Introduction

How to convince anyone to do anything

Persuasion is not debate. You aren't trying to pick out flaws in someone's argument or prove to them that they are wrong or deluded. Even if they admit they are wrong, that doesn't necessarily mean you have won them over to your way of thinking. That's something completely different. That's persuasion, and it happens to be a virtue—as long as it is used properly. It could easily become a vice if used improperly, because you could also persuade someone to do something that is wrong or not in their best interest. So how do we use persuasion properly? How do we ensure we are using it virtuously? Let's find out now.

 With the virtue of persuasiveness, you have the power to convince people to do something different. You're a great negotiator and use compelling, passionate arguments to get what you want. You are influential and motivational, knowing how to push the right buttons to promote a particular agenda.

To acquire more of this virtue, first, we need to learn Greek. We will look to Aristotle, the classical Greek philosopher, to learn more about the importance of combining ethos, pathos, and logos to create a persuasive article, speech, or presentation so that we are more convincing to anyone. While actually learning Greek might not be a practical approach for everyone, understanding the essence of Aristotle's teachings and applying them to our communication strategies will undoubtedly enhance our persuasive abilities.

Next, we need to target someone's values. One-on-one influence is easier to achieve when you know the temperament of your listener. To persuade effectively, all you do is to set aside your own colorized preferences and adopt the perspectives of your listener. How do you do that? Well, that's what we'll discuss.

Next, we need to speak colorfully. After you have adjusted your pitch to accommodate the core values of the different temperaments, you should also consider using words or phrases that reflect those values. This section will also review the communication styles of each color.

Next, we need to watch our tone. Your tone indicates your attitude towards a certain topic or subject, helps set the mood, and elicits certain thoughts and feelings. Sometimes it's not about what you say, but rather the way you say it, and the impression it makes on everyone in your audience who reads or hears you.

Next, we need to try to engage everyone. Once we've mastered the one-to-one persuasion process, it's time to advance to figuring out how to work one-to-many. This requires us to adjust our message so that we appeal, at some level, to all four colors. One easy way to connect to all four types is use the four E's of engagement, which we'll explore in this section.

Finally, we need to avoid manipulation. This is when you intentionally exploit your understanding of others or their circumstances to get them to believe or do something that benefits you more than it benefits them. Many books have been written that teach people how to do exactly this. We will learn how to avoid manipulation like a deadly virus, because if we don't, we will destroy our relationships.

Once we regularly follow and practice these six strategies, we will not only become more persuasive, but we will also develop a keen sense of awareness when someone is attempting to persuade us. This heightened understanding allows us to critically evaluate the intentions behind their messages and discern whether their appeals align with our values and virtues. If we find that they are trying to get us to do something that isn't virtuous, we'll be able to resist their influence and maintain our freedom of thought and self-control. Cultivating this important skill will empower us to make informed decisions, avoid manipulative tactics, and stay true to our core beliefs. Furthermore, it enables us to engage in meaningful conversations, fostering understanding and cooperation among diverse individuals. As we embark on this journey together, I look forward to working with you in honing this essential skill, and witnessing the transformative impact it has on our lives and the world around us.

Lesson 1

Learn Greek

Aristotle is one of the big three ancient Greek philosophers who laid the foundation for logic and the modern scientific method. He also defined the essential elements of ethics, aesthetics, poetics, metaphysics, and politics. One of his books was entitled, *On Rhetoric,* in which he explains his theories of persuasive language and speech. In particular, he expounded on the concepts of ethos, pathos, and logos, which are not the names of Dumas' *Three Musketeers*.

Ethos is the Greek word for "custom" or "character." Whenever we try to convince someone about the reliability of our character, declare our authority, or establish the credibility of our argument, we are appealing to ethos. It is what makes us worthy of trust. It is related to the study of ethics and morals, which tries to figure out what is good or bad for society. Ethos is what persuades you to eliminate vice and champion virtue in your life because you believe it is the right thing to do for yourself and our society at large.

Pathos is the Greek word for "emotion," "suffering," or "experience." If we try to evoke an emotional response in our audience as we try to persuade them to do something, we are using pathos. Perhaps we try to appeal to their hopes and dreams, or play on their fears and worries, or support their beliefs, values, or temperament preferences. This emotional appeal extends to our senses: if we make the presentation aesthetically pleasing to watch, enjoyable to listen to, and fun or entertaining to experience, it will be more persuasive.

Logos is Greek for "reason" which, according to Aristotle, is the controlling principle in the universe. Aristotle was likely an extroverted Green with Gold as his secondary color, which may explain why he believes the "left-brained" functions of logic and reason are more important than ethics and feelings. We wouldn't expect him to think otherwise. More modern research indicates that an appeal to ethos and pathos affects more people than an appeal to logos, which aligns with what we know about temperament distributions where the logical Green comprises less than 10% of the general population.

> "In Aristotelian terms, the good leader must have ethos, pathos and logos. The ethos is his moral character, the source of his ability to persuade. The pathos is his ability to touch feelings to move people emotionally. The logos is his ability to give solid reasons for an action, to move people intellectually."
>
> —Mortimer Adler

When we intentionally combine all three of these elements into a persuasive article, speech, or presentation, we are more convincing to everyone. To incorporate ethos, remind the audience on who you are and why you are an authority on the subject. Make sure you use credible or authoritative sources if you aren't an authority. At the very least, use correct grammar, jargon, and language to sound credible and trustworthy. For pathos, try to use descriptive language or imagery that evokes emotion. Telling personal stories is a great strategy as appealing to your shared values. Bring as much genuine energy and passion into your presentation as you can without going overboard. To incorporate logos, use research, statistics, and convincing, solid evidence to back up your claims. Keep your argument clear and logical, carefully leading the audience to your conclusion.

Aristotle's teachings on ethos, pathos, and logos provide a timeless framework for effective communication and persuasion. By understanding and incorporating these three elements, we can create powerful and persuasive messages that resonate with diverse audiences. By establishing credibility through ethos, evoking emotion through pathos, and presenting solid reasoning through logos, we can engage and persuade people on a deeper level, fostering understanding and inspiring change.

In today's fast-paced world, it is more important than ever to communicate effectively and meaningfully. By following Aristotle's wisdom and mastering the art of persuasion, we can not only enrich our own lives but also contribute positively to the world around us. So, as we continue to learn and grow, let us embrace the teachings of this great philosopher and strive to become skilled communicators who can navigate the complexities of human interaction with empathy, intelligence, and eloquence. By doing so, we can truly make a difference in our personal lives, our communities, and our society at large.

Assignments

🖉 1A: Why is it important to know the interests, prejudices, and expectations of your audience?

🖉 1B: If two speakers are debating each other, and they have identical credentials, the one who is more relatable will win over the audience. How can you become more relatable?

🖉 1C: Write a persuasive paragraph where you try to appeal to ethos, pathos, and logos.

Lesson 2

Target values

One-on-one influence is easier to achieve when you know the temperament of your listener. To persuade effectively, all you do is to set aside your own colorized preferences and adopt the perspectives of your listener. This is often easier said than done especially if your primary color is substantially stronger than then other colors in your spectrum. But if you spend enough time consciously trying to see the world through the lenses of the person you are trying to persuade, you will find success.

Adopting the perspectives of your audience allows you to frame your presentation in a way that accommodates the values of your listener. As you discuss the consequences of accepting or rejecting your offer, ensure those consequences reflect their values as much as possible. To help you remember what those values are, here is a quick review:

- Blue: acceptance, causes, comfort, communication, empathy, feelings, growth, harmony, integrity, intimacy, kindness, meaning, relationships, romance, uniqueness
- Gold: achievement, appreciation, authority, completion, dedication, discipline, order, organizations, power, prudence, responsibilities, rules, security, structure, traditions
- Green: analysis, autonomy, competence, composure, data, debates, efficiency, genius, information, innovation, mysteries, solutions, technology, time, understanding
- Orange: action, activities, adventure, challenges, courage, excitement, experiences, freedom, impulses, incentives, recreation, skill, success, talent, victory

Let's look at what this might look like. Suppose you were trying to persuade a Gold person to buy an expensive luxury car. Because you understand what they value most in life, you know that they are likely to be concerned with its warranty, safety mechanisms, fuel efficiency, financing options, security system, maintenance schedule, and reliability. Will this investment pay off in terms of increasing their social status or projecting the image that its owner is a hard-working and powerful member of society? Will the car have a higher resale value than others? Is the seller polite, punctual, and professional? Is the seller well-groomed, well-organized, and well-behaved? Does the dealership have a good reputation? Will the car consistently get you where you need to be when you need to be there? If it doesn't, and needs to be repaired, will the dealership provide a temporary replacement? Is it available in traditional, conservative colors? Will the seller make accommodations, offer discounts, or provide bonus benefits? These are the types of things a Gold buyer will want to see because they reflect the Gold's values. If they don't see them, they are unlikely to buy.

> "Approach each customer with the idea of helping him or her to solve a problem or achieve a goal, not of selling a product or service."
>
> —Brian Tracy

Assignments

✎ 2A: How would you sell a luxury car to a Blue buyer?

✎ 2B: How would you sell a luxury car to a Green buyer?

✎ 2C: How would you sell a luxury car to an Orange buyer?

✎ 2D: What are ways you can identify a stranger's temperament so you can alter your pitch to target their values?

Lesson 3

Speak colorfully

After you have adjusted your pitch to accommodate the core values of the different temperaments, you should also consider using words or phrases that reflect those values.

- Blues use the unification and relating language that guides their lives. They imbue their language with embracing, encompassing, empowering words such as *associate, collect, combine, fuse, integrate, unite*. Blues also describe the world in terms of emotions, like *harmony, mystical, wonder, care for*, or of relationships, including *love, marry, feel, attract, clasp, bond*.

- Gold speech often includes short, imperative command words, such as *check, keep, lock, do, go*. Golds also reveal their fondness for rules and procedures through frequent use of words such as *proper, regular, regulate, right, comply, organize*, and their motivation to higher causes by words such as *duty, honor, sacrifice, protect, serve*.

- Green speech carries with it a detached air of analysis, with judgment getting closer, but always reserved in case more data comes in: *analyze, measure, inspect, look it over, test*. Greens also use words that indicate intellectual processes: *critique, classify, arrange, sort, sift*, as well as terms dealing with discussion, such as *debate, argue, question, challenge, prove*.

- Orange speech tends to focus on what can be sensed, with words like *explode, fly, feel, see, ride, catch, float, thump, tingle, soar, dazzle*. They pepper their speech with enthusiastic verbs, such as *create, set up, dream, envision, cause, liven up*, and words that have a tinge of hope, such as *believe, imagine, hint, wonder, suspect*.

Communication styles

In addition to having their own values which determines *what* you should talk about as well as the words to use, each temperament has their own way of communicating. If you want to connect to that temperament, then you also need to change *how* you communicate with that person.

Blue

- Be genuine and sincere.
- Be sensitive to body language.
- Express feelings and emotions.
- Listen intently.
- Maintain eye contact.
- Avoid debate or conflict.
- Show empathy and concern.

Gold

- Appreciate their time.
- Stay orderly and on task.
- Be courteous and polite.
- Be direct and professional.
- Talk about expectations.
- Turn solutions into actions.
- Be authoritative if justified.

Green

- Talk about possibilities.
- Stay unemotional.
- Expect skepticism or debate.
- Remain factual and logical.
- Avoid small talk.

- Allow for questions.
- Give them time to think.

Orange

- Be bold and confident.
- Talk about past experiences.
- Use ordinary language.
- Talk in concrete terms.
- Focus on action and results.
- Be interesting and energetic.
- Be honest and direct.

> "Misunderstandings happen because we do not understand that different people have different styles of communication."
>
> —Tony Alessandra

Assignments

🖉 3A: How do you prefer someone to talk with you? Describe what this looks like.

🖉 3B: What if you can't identify someone's temperament? What should you do in this circumstance?

Lesson 4

Watch your tone

As you attempt to persuade others, you need to consider your audience and the overall tone of your message. Your tone indicates your attitude towards a certain topic or subject, helps set the mood, and elicits certain thoughts and feelings. Sometimes it's not about what you say, but rather the way you say it, and the impression it makes on everyone in your audience who reads or hears you. Using the wrong tone will likely cause them to entirely ignore your message.

> "We often refuse to accept an idea merely because the tone of voice in which it has been expressed is unsympathetic to us."
>
> —Friedrich Nietzsche

Some personalities appreciate some tones more than others because they align with the way they prefer to communicate. Just as you would deliver a message differently to a group of children than you would to a group of aging academics, you need to alter the overall tone of your presentation based on the temperaments or preferences of your audience. If you don't know the preferences of your audience, or are speaking to a group of mixed temperaments, then you can get away with using multiple tones to appeal to different people at different times. But if you are trying to persuade someone one-on-one, the more you want to alter your message to appeal to the tones of voice they prefer—not the tones you prefer.

Below is a list of the tones that reflect the values of each temperament. These should be your default, go-to choices when interacting with these types. Of course, there are times when you may want to use a different tone, especially in situations where you require immediate action.

Blue Tones

Agreeable, benevolent, inspirational, grateful, caring, tactful, eloquent, pleading, imploring, tenderly, kind, understanding, supportive, sensitive, emotional, well-meaning, accommodating, hopeful, reflective, forgiving, nostalgic, familiar, compassionate, conciliatory, warm-hearted, unprejudiced, considerate, reassuring, appreciative, trusting, sincere, subjective, intimate, conversational, empathetic, sentimental, sympathetic, confidential, honest, gentle, patient, encouraging, praising, charitable, tolerant.

Gold Tones

Powerful, guarding, proper, intense, cautionary, approving, worried, honor, obedient, reminding, apprehensive, solemn, fair, concerned, stressed, shielding, lawful, strong-willed, recommending, reminiscent, earnest, dignified, desirable, diplomatic, respectful, plain-spoken, urgent, assertive, moral, watchful, formal, forceful, reverential, upstanding, deferential, authoritative, realistic, determined, insistent, respected, commanding, instructive, controlled, serious, righteous.

Green Tones

Neutral, unbiased, ironic, theoretical, questioning, edgy, complex, informative, objective, cryptic, restrained, witty, doubtful, pragmatic, curious, educational, introspective, inquisitive, confident, matter-of-fact, contemplative, cool, logical, influential, self-confident, calm, rational, concentrated, fascinating, rhetorical, indifferent, truthful, doubting, unconvinced, mindful, detached, sensible, factual, perplexed, plausible, clever, distant, impartial, open-minded, analytical.

Orange Tones

Sensationalistic, provocative, bold, offbeat, happy, animated, flexible, flashy, generous, energetic, high-spirited, courageous, unreserved, carefree, impassioned, straightforward, joyful, relaxed, spirited, entertaining, persuasive, celebratory, vibrant, jubilant, light-hearted, cheery, lively, grandiose, informal, humorous, undaunted, daring, jesting, playful, optimistic, aroused, enthusiastic, convincing, frank, excited, lenient, amused, candid, ecstatic, passionate.

Assignments

🖉 4A: When someone talks with you, how do you prefer them to communicate with you? Which tones do you like to hear?

🖉 4B: If you know someone's temperament, practice using one of the tones that appeal to their primary color. Halfway through your presentation, switch to a tone from their least dominant color. Describe the difference between the two reactions.

🖉 4C: The list above intentionally identifies positive tones. But what is positive for one temperament may be negative to another. Provide a couple of examples of this issue.

Lesson 5

Engage everyone

Once we've mastered the one-to-one persuasion process, it's time to advance to figuring out how to work one-to-many. This requires us to adjust our message so that we appeal, at some level, to all four colors. One easy way to connect to all four types is use the four E's of engagement:

Edify. Blues need to be edified—the more uplifting and emotional their experience, the more they retain and the more they are influenced. For example, Blues want personal stories and examples, such as "My wife and child the other day...." And they appreciate some personal disclosure of feelings or intimate thoughts. They must see the humanness of the speaker—culminating in a sob or a lump in the throat if possible. In fact, for the most profound impact, Blues must have an emotional experience. They must see how this idea or principle can make their life better. They love adjectives and vivid descriptions. They like symbols, poems, and poetic devices. They like to hear changes in the speaker's vocal pitch, volume, and inflection. They love dramatic pauses. These things keep them involved emotionally.

Empower. Golds seek empowerment—their parts of the presentation should leave them better able to control and organize their world. For example, make sure that the organization of your materials is evident. Perhaps you can use a point-by-point system. This facilitates organized note taking and shouts, "I'm following a structure!" It was probably a Gold who first said that to give a good speech, you must, "tell 'em what you're gonna tell 'em, tell 'em, then tell 'em what you told 'em." They like lists of things to do and ways to gauge their progress in accomplishing those things. They want to hear about standards, benchmarks, policies, procedures, and values.

Enlighten. Greens need to be enlightened—they must feel they're trading their time for something new that will increase their capabilities. For example, Greens critically evaluate nearly every statement. Don't be afraid to call in authorities; better yet, call an authority before you speak, bounce as many of your ideas off that person as you can before they hang up on you, and then say to your audience, "I was speaking to Ralph Obergnan the other day. Ralph is the Chief Information Officer for the XYZ Corporation, and he says that...." Now you're speaking as someone who knows Ralph. As long as you aren't incoherent, redundant, or rambling, Greens are fairly tolerant of tangential thoughts, especially if they hear some little-known fact or figure they can assimilate and spit out some-where else. They like puns and witticisms. They admire arcane analogies, amusing anecdotes, astute anachronisms, and artful alliteration. And Greens love those "a-haa!" moments. Keep them thinking, guessing, and intellectually involved, and you can win over this tough segment.

Entertain. Oranges need to be entertained—let them have a good time. If you can be funny, try and connect with your Oranges, who often live from joke to joke. Active gestures, passionate theatrics, and melodrama will usually get the point across better than a dozen union enforcers with billy clubs. Oranges also want to move from point to point as quickly as possible. And the points must be unambiguous and memorable. They enjoy sensational stories, particularly those that appeal to their values, like heroism and chutzpah. They must be able to see how they can apply the information in real time and in real life. Try to script in visual aids or engaging multimedia. Speak with style, with flair, with charisma, with energy. Keep them entertained.

As you use the four E's in speaking one-to-many, be a little bee. Bounce from flower to flower, trying to keep all the temperaments involved. An Orange joke here, a quote from a Gold authority or outline there, a Green term now and then, and an inspirational story for the Blues. Because everyone is a blend of all four temperament, even if you don't connect directly to your listener's primary style, you may still hook up via a secondary one.

"People will do anything for those who encourage their dreams, justify their failures, allay their fears, confirm their suspicions, and help them throw rocks at their enemies."

—Blair Warren

Assignments

- 5A: Identify a speech, presentation, or advertisement that appeals to at least one color. Which temperament does it target and how does it do it?

- 5B: Identify a speech, presentation, or advertisement that appeals to all four temperaments. Is it effective? Why or why not?

- 5C: Develop your own speech, presentation, or advertisement that appeals to all four temperaments with different sections that edify, empower, enlighten, and entertain.

Lesson 6

Avoid manipulation

The more we learn about human nature, especially temperament, the more we learn how to successfully communicate and motivate those around us because we try to communicate in ways they prefer, talk about topics they want to discuss, and shape our interactions around their values and preferences. This intentional effort to thoughtfully connect produces a degree of trust and confidence that strengthens your relationship and enhances their opinion of you. It becomes a powerful tool in our efforts to influence others to change their attitudes, beliefs, or behaviors. But just like any other tool, it can be used for good or evil purposes.

> "We happen to live in an era that is incredibly wrapped up in notions of political correctness; everything is seen through the lens of politics. But being political and politically correct is just another way of fighting, another form of power and strategy, an insidious means of manipulation."
>
> —Robert Greene

Persuasion is the skill of encouraging others to believe or do something that usually leads them to obtain positive results. Your intention is to teach them what you have learned to provide a meaningful benefit in their lives. Notice the focus is to help them or help society in general. Manipulation, on the other hand, is when you intentionally exploit your understanding of others or their circumstances to get them to believe or do something that benefits you more than it benefits them. Manipulators are victimizers, cause more harm than good, and end up destroying their shallow, counterfeit relationships. Being persuasive is a hallmark of someone with a mature and moral understanding of temperament, while being manipulative reflects immaturity and immorality.

In 1998, Robert Greene published *The 48 Laws of Power,* a controversial book that would become an international bestseller and the first of a series of Machiavellian books that explain how to manipulate others to do what you want them to do. Greene suggested that his books should be used to not only obtain more power but also recognize when others are using those techniques against you. Some of its "laws" include the following items:

- Never outshine the master; make those above you feel superior.
- Crush your enemy totally.
- When asking for help, appeal to people's self-interest.
- Create compelling spectacles.
- Make other people come to you; use bait if necessary.
- Keep others in suspended terror.
- Think as you like but behave like others.
- Destroy enemies by attacking their reputation.
- Do not commit to anyone.
- Create a cult-like following.
- Let others to do the work for you, but always take credit.
- Seduce others by operating on their individual psychologies and weaknesses.
- Strike the shepherd and the sheep will scatter.

The Orange Virtues

- Learn to keep people dependent on you.
- Pose as a friend, work as a spy.
- Use selective honesty and generosity to disarm your victim.
- Always say less than necessary.
- Court attention at all cost.
- Discover each person's thumbscrew.
- Conceal your intentions.
- Play a sucker to catch a sucker.
- Play to people's fantasies.

Assignments

- 6A: As you read through Green's advice on how to manipulate others, what was going on in your heart and mind?

- 6B: Have you ever been manipulated by others? If so, what techniques were used against you?

- 6C: How do you know when you have crossed the line from being persuasive to being manipulative?

- 6D: What is your commitment to never use manipulative techniques to try to get ahead at the expense of others?

Introduction

Why exhibiting playfulness will stop you from freaking out

If you would like to tap into a new source of creative fuel, if you would like to make it easier to learn, if you want to quickly solve challenging problems, if you want to reduce stress and tension, if you want to foster empathy, compassion, trust, and intimacy—then join me as we learn how to become more *playful*. It is a virtue. And we all need more of it.

> With the virtue of playfulness, you can take an activity that is dull and boring and turn it into something that is far more joyful, fun, and enjoyable. You have a pleasant sense of humor and enjoy the funny side of life. You like to party, flirt, frolic, and play merry pranks with your friends. You crave opportunities to have a good time.

How do we become more playful or incorporate playfulness into our lives? Here are six simple steps for starters.

First, liberate your imagination. Playfulness is what allows us to turn the world upside down and see everything in a new way. It gives us flexibility and allows us to see the options that were previously hidden and could only be viewed from an unusual perspective, like the one you get when you bend over and peek at the up-side down and backwards world between your legs.

Second, playfully explore. What kinds of things did you like to investigate when you were a child? What would you like to explore as an adult? How can you be more playful in your explorations? What are you going to do to explore possibilities more fully?

Third, enjoy dizzying fun. When was the last time you dislodged calcium carbonate crystals in the otolithic organs of the inner ear that affected your vestibular system and its balancing mechanisms? What are some safe and acceptable ways that you can physically play to enjoy the dizzy, giddy, and zippy moments of life?

Fourth, ungag your humor. Regardless of whether you giggle, titter, snicker, snort, chuckle, chortle, cackle, bray, or have a side-splitting belly laugh, you should know that laughter is one of the therapeutic secrets to happiness and well-being. What makes you laugh the hardest?

Fifth, clown around. Rather than relying on vocalized words, clowns communicate through their body language: posture, gesture, contortion, touch, location, movement, and the thousands of expressions that can be made with the 43 different muscles in our face. In the reading, we'll discover how to clown around effectively.

Sixth, play colorfully. Looking at playfulness through the lens of human temperament, we understand that different temperaments have different ways of spending their play time. Most of the time, the activities they consider to be fun reflect their values and preferences. We'll make some lists of playful activities that appeal to each color.

The virtue of playfulness allows us to turn something that is normally dull and boring into something that is far more joyful, fun, and enjoyable. Let's sacrifice our internal fuddy-duddy and practice, then perfect, our playfulness.

Lesson 1

Liberate your imagination

Playfulness is a critical component of creativity and imagination. It is what allows us to turn the world upside down and see everything in a new way. It gives us flexibility and allows us to see the options that were previously hidden and could only be viewed from an unusual perspective, like the one you get when you bend over and peek at the upside down and backwards world between your legs. It gives us fluid thinking—the ability to think outside the box and connect the dots between multiple concepts in unique and creative ways. Not only do we see people, places, and things in newfangled ways, but we are able to express those to others, inviting them into our unique and imaginative world. It may be a pretend place like Middle Earth, Narnia, Tatooine, Hogwarts, Asgard, Pandora, or Gotham City, but these worlds have been explored by hundreds of millions of people, who have shelved out billions of dollars to experience them for themselves.

Looking at the world with playful imagination allows you to invent new words, such as Lewis Carroll's poem *Jabberwocky* which introduced the word *chortle* to the English language or Roald Dahl's *scrumdiddlyumptious* and its antonym *uckyslush*. If you are a fan of the Assassin's Creed video game series, you may be familiar with the mysterious language of Isu, which is a constructed language with not only vocabulary, but rules of grammar and phonology as well. Today you can learn Klingon in case you ever visit the Star Trek universe, Newspeak if you think you are living in George Orwell's totalitarian dystopia, or join the two million people around the world who speak Esperanto, the international language designed in the 1870s to foster harmony between people from different countries. In fact, if you want to quickly get rid of pesky telemarketers and door-to-door hucksters, invent your own nonsense language on-the-fly to bring an end to intrusive conversations.

By tapping into your imagination, you can create your own poetry, brand logos, dance movements, inventions, artwork, songs, clothing, plays, furniture, household gadgets, decorations, videos, recipes, quilts, advertisements, processes, stories, vehicles, podcasts, games, product reviews, sound effects, businesses, perfume, mementos, tools, and so on. You can also take up and reshape cultural experiences, create social spaces, change public opinions, develop alternative systems of power and control, champion causes, invent shared narratives, launch political movements, enhance interpersonal relationships, and transform possibilities into reality. There are no limits to your imagination and the things you can accomplish when you put it to good use.

> "Imagination will often carry us to worlds that never were. But without it we go nowhere."
>
> —Carl Sagan

Assignments

🖉 1A: Who are some people that had an idea and then built on it to change the world? Explain their contributions.

🖉 1B: Why are successful people successful? What qualities do they possess that you want to possess?

🖉 1C: Identify an everyday object, such as a chair. Now think of at least ten things or processes that the object could symbolize.

🖉 1D: Using your imagination, think of some ways you can be a positive influencer for good.

Lesson 2

Playfully explore

Playfulness allows you to explore the world around you and solve problems that you wouldn't have otherwise been able to solve. If you take the time to explore and investigate the properties of the objects around you, you might be able to spot some imperfections or ways to enhance those items. For example, in 1874 a US patent was issued to medical doctor Samuel Francis who had been trying to figure out a way to reduce the number of table utensils someone uses to eat. He combined the knife, fork, and spoon into a single utensil, now known as the *sporknife* or *knispork*. In patent US147119A, he described it like this: "I form the knife on one edge of the spoon-bowl, while the fork-tines are placed at the front end of said bowl." Among other things, he also invented a toothbrush with rubber bristles, a matchbox that lit a match from the inside, a type of instant tea, new kinds of sleds, glass-based burn treatments, a cane with a hidden compartment to store your bus fare, a typewriter that looked like a piano, a postage-canceling device, and a self-opening coffin in case you were buried alive.

> "Put a picture of yourself as a child in view somewhere, to remind yourself to be playful."
>
> —Alexandra Stoddard

As you work on solving problems, it helps to play around with what we think we know to be true. Or perhaps you explore the nature of opposites, such as action and reaction, cause and effect, sorting and matching, sizing and ordering, sequencing and grouping, and similarities and differences. Or perhaps you can combine elements that haven't been tried before. Rather than sitting back and theorizing what might happen, these hands-on investigators would rather experiment and see what happens. Would people enjoy a hamburger with peanut butter instead of cheese? Can you breed a goat and a sheep together to create a new *geep* hybrid? If a shopping mall wanted to reduce its number of teenage loiterers, would blasting opera music through its loudspeakers drive them out? What if we installed two dishwashers into a kitchen instead of one so you could grab clean dishes out of one and put dirty dishes in the other—no more need for shelves.

In thinking about how to be more playful as you explore the world around you, consider adopting the following behaviors:

- Think about alternative uses to common products.
- Question why we do things the way we do.
- Make your thinking visible or understandable to others.
- Turn a one-function device into a multi-functioned device.
- See if you can get different outcomes than what is expected.
- Test limits in a safe and responsible manner.
- Form hypotheses about how and why things happen.
- Work with others to make plans and decisions.
- Exercise your powers of observation.
- Turn something into a competition then play fairly.
- Test your strength, speed, agility, or control.
- Choose from a range of materials and tools.
- Explore different roles and responsibilities.
- Invent approaches to practical problems.
- Use all your senses to explore the world.
- Make substitutions and trade-offs.

- Set aside reality and explore possibilities.

Assignments

✐ 2A: As a child, what kinds of things did you like to explore or investigate?

✐ 2B: As an adult, what kinds of things would you like to explore or investigate?

✐ 2C: How do you plan to be more playful in your explorations?

Lesson 3

Enjoy dizzying fun

Remember when you were a child and loved spinning around, riding a merry-go-round, flying high on a swing, or going up and down on a teeter-totter? Perhaps you rolled down a grass-lined hill, performed handstands, cartwheels, and somersaults, swung upside-down on monkey bars, slid down slides, jumped on trampolines, twirled jump ropes, or rode a rocking-horse. Why has something that we once loved to do as children, now morphed into a nauseating, vertigo-inducing experience?

Perhaps it has something to do with the dislodged calcium carbonate crystals in the otolithic organs of the inner ear that affect our vestibular system and its balancing mechanisms. Perhaps it is because we are unhealthy or debilitated in some way. Perhaps it is because we are afraid of breaking our increasingly-brittle bones or incurring some sort of debilitating spinal injury. Or perhaps it is because we rarely see adults playing on the equipment at the neighborhood park, look strangely at them if they are, and cautiously reign in our children if they wander too close to the obviously deviant adult. It seems that at some point in time, we determined it was simply too childish for adults to do those sorts of things. But is it? Don't we still crave those dizzying, physical sensations?

There is a reason that millions of fully-grown adults spend billions of hard-earned dollars at amusement parks to ride whirling attractions, gyrating simulators, and maniacal roller-coasters that induce these feelings, or why they spend their weekends speeding down ski slopes, pedaling up and down mountain paths, free climbing up rocky cliffs, racing around in motorized off-road vehicles, skydiving out of airplanes, bungee jumping, sliding down zip lines, rafting down white-water rapids, and so on. Many adventurous recreational activities induce some sort of pleasant physical sensation as we feel like we are living on the edge. It appears like the more we do them, the more we crave them because these dizzying activities release adrenaline, dopamine, and other chemicals that cause a feeling of exhilaration, pleasure, well-being, accomplishment, and peace.

The need for physical play sometimes takes the form of rough and tumble play. We certainly see this in youngsters as they are learning how their bodies work and what they can and cannot do, or what they should or should not do. But we also see it in adults. Consider the wide-scale acceptance of more violent or aggressive sports such as rugby, hockey, boxing, mixed martial arts, wrestling, basketball, and American football. Whether you're a spectator or a participant, as the scores grow similar to each other, feelings are heightened, and passions are aroused. It often makes the game more intense and interactive as our central nervous system releases neurochemicals or as tipsy observers imbibe more liquid chemicals. It seems many of us are biologically wired to enjoy sports or games where we compete to disrupt the order or equilibrium of a system, and then restore or rebuild it more to our liking, which is what happens when our team or our favorite champion moves up in the rankings.

> "As long as the world is turning and spinning, we're gonna be dizzy and we're gonna make mistakes."
>
> —Mel Brooks

Assignments

✏ 3A: What are some safe and acceptable ways that you can physically play to enjoy the dizzy, giddy, and zippy moments?

✏ 3B: Do you spend enough time doing physically fun things? Why or why not?

✏ 3C: If we can't have as much fun as we desire physically, sometimes we engage in alternatives behaviors that aren't healthy to ourselves or our relationships. Identify some alternatives that have appealed to you or those around you.

✏ 3D: What can you do to help someone who engages in behaviors or habits that might be pleasurable but harmful to them or others?

Lesson 4

Ungag your humor

Regardless of whether you giggle, titter, snicker, snort, chuckle, chortle, cackle, bray, or have a side-splitting belly laugh, you have discovered that laughter is one of the therapeutic secrets to happiness and well-being. Unless you suffer from *gelotophobia*, or the fear of laughter, don't shy away from things that tickle your funny bone. In fact, besides improving your mood, daily doses of laughter may keep your heart stronger, lower blood sugar levels, relieve stress, soothe tension, relieve pain, and strengthen the immune system. Laughter is good medicine.

"The early bird gets the worm, but the second mouse gets the cheese."

—Steven Wright

In the aftermath of the 9/11 terrorist attacks, the British Association for the Advancement of Science, under the direction of experimental psychologist and magician, Richard Wiseman, devised the *LaughLab* project to identify the world's funniest joke—one that retained its funniness across cultural and political boundaries. For over a year they systematically studied jokes and gathered rankings until they finally declared the international winner:

> Two hunters are out in the woods when one of them collapses. He doesn't seem to be breathing and his eyes are glazed. The other guy whips out his phone and calls the emergency services. He gasps, "My friend is dead! What can I do?" The operator says, "Calm down. I can help. First, let's make sure he's dead." There is a silence; then a gunshot is heard. Back on the phone, the guy says, "OK, now what?"

In America, the winner was:

> A man and a friend are playing golf one day at their local golf course. One of the guys is about to chip onto the green when he sees a long funeral procession on the road next to the course. He stops in mid-swing, takes off his golf cap, closes his eyes, and bows down in prayer. His friend says: "Wow, that is the most thoughtful and touching thing I have ever seen. You truly are a kind man." The man then replies: "Yeah, well we were married 35 years."

According to the philosophical pessimist Arthur Schopenhauer, we are amused when we are surprised by something that is incongruent or absurd. We see that in the old joke: Two fish are in a tank. One says to the other, "Do you know how to drive this thing?" When we read the first sentence, we imagine a fish tank. But in the second, we realize they are talking about a military tank. It is funny because it is absurd to think of talking fish who are trying to drive a military tank. It shakes up our expectations and engages our imagination.

Sometimes we laugh at others because it makes us feel superior to them. This happens when comedians make fun of themselves, their family, or their heritage. But when they make fun of others because of some characteristic that differentiates them from others, and you also possess that characteristic, it stops being funny. History is filled with mean-spirited or cruel jokes that represent one group's attempt at making fun of another group who possesses a different gender, race, intelligence, beauty, sexual preference, temperament, etc. Laughing at the expense of others isn't humor—it is hate-filled hubris.

Assignments

🖉 4A: Humor can be learned. Make a commitment to learn and repeat at least one new joke or pun each day. What is your favorite joke?

🖉 4B: Who or what makes you laugh the hardest? Explain.

🖉 4C: Is a sense of humor important to a successful relationship? Explain.

🖉 4D: Find a way to laugh about your own situations, even if you start off by forcing a laugh. How does it affect your stress?

🖉 4E: Some jokes are funny to someone but unfunny to someone else. Think of at least five reasons why this is true.

🖉 4F: Others believe that laughing, disparaging, or demeaning someone outside of your in-group is funny. But is it? Do you laugh because you feel superior?

Lesson 5

Clown around

A comedian is someone who tells funny jokes and amusing anecdotes while a clown is someone who is funny and amusing to watch. Rather than relying on vocalized words, clowns communicate through their body language: posture, gesture, contortion, touch, location, movement, and the thousands of expressions that can be made with the 43 different muscles in our face. When you supplement that with props, gags, makeup, and costumes, you transform into a clown. Great clowns can improvise and adapt their act to meet the moods of their audience, portraying silly and fun characters as well as those who are sad and poignant, as in the case of Charlie Chaplin's *Little Tramp* character. The job of a clown isn't necessarily to make you laugh or cry, but to make you feel something, and feel it deeply.

Clowns are great at maintaining continuous eye contact to keep their audience engaged. Some clowns follow the rule of complete silence to ensure their bodies are doing the talking. When a clown faces a problem, even though the audience can easily spot the solution, the clown cannot. It is in the space between the problem and the solution where the clowning occurs. We laugh at their honest, earnest, struggling antics and their growing frustration and desperation. Each time the problem is about to be solved it deteriorates into an increasingly worse problem. This continues until the act ends in a surprising or unexpected payoff. Clowns are completely honest and transparent because everything they feel or think is clearly visible to the audience, regardless of their age.

Why are we talking about clowns? Because the exaggerated expressions, the unpredictable behaviors, the desire to communicate every thought and emotion through subtle and not-so-subtle body language, demands the level of playfulness and creativity that we are seeking to develop. Tapping into your internal clown, trying to honestly express your ideas and struggles through play, requires thinking about the world and your relationships in a different way. Of course, the essence of a clown does not lie in cracking jokes, walking around in big shoes, or throwing a cream pie into someone's face. A clown is not a role you learn and act out: it is an attitude. In fact, clowns possess five attitudes that anyone can adopt, even those who are habitual sourpusses:

> "I've had great success being a total idiot."
>
> —Jerry Lewis

First, clowns are committed to their craft. They love it and want to succeed in it. They focus on their performance and maintain control of every nuance, every motion, every thought. They are completely "in the moment" and adjust their performance as the job requires, always keeping their audience squarely in mind.

Second, they turn their work into play. Even the boring and dull becomes exciting and sharp. They inject fun into everything they can, adding whimsy, humor, exaggeration, anticipation, and entertainment every place they can. Because work is now play, they play with complete gusto and wild abandonment. They understand that when people start to feel stressed out, efficiency, productivity, and happiness go spiraling down the drain, but when they feel relaxed, happy, and playful, they tend to get much more work done.

Third, clowns are team players who work with everyone in their troop, regardless of their differences. In fact, they celebrate those differences and play off them, creating new stories and new interactions with every performance. Everyone's unique strengths are spotlighted and used along the way, working together to produce more than the sum of their parts.

Fourth, clowns remain positive and upbeat, even when struggling with an impossible problem. They understand that failure is always a part of the path to success, and leads to temporary setbacks, most of which can be laughed off from a different perspective. Despite obstacles, even absurd ones, they never lose their positivity, keeping the smile painted on their face, helping others finding joy in the journey, overcoming challenges in surprising and unexpected ways.

Fifth, clowns intentionally form emotional connections with their audience. These bonds are made more intense because of the transparency and vulnerability that is offered by the clown, who is willing to face humiliation and embarrassment by acting silly and ridiculous in front of a others, just because they want others to have a happier day.

Assignments

✏ 5A: List some television or movie stars who are known for their ability to clown around.

✏ 5B: Why are people hesitant to clown around and introduce laughter and humor into their world?

✏ 5C: What specific things are you going to do to embrace your inner clown?

Lesson 6

Play colorfully

Looking at playfulness through the lens of human temperament, we understand that different temperaments have different ways of spending their play time. Most of the time, the activities they consider to be fun reflect their values and preferences. For example, a fun weekend for Golds who value orderliness may be to spend the entire time reorganizing their garage, placing all their bits and bobs into neatly labeled bins and boxes. But non-Golds are likely to find this chore to be the opposite of fun and more like a death sentence. Therefore, as we interact with others and invite them to be more playful, we should help them play in ways that are meaningful to them, or better yet, join with them as they play in ways they prefer, rather than in ways we prefer.

Blues

Blue leisure activities usually involve their close circle of friends or family. It doesn't matter what they do, just as long as they do it together and take advantage of the time to strengthen their relationships. When they want to be by themselves, they read novels, listen to music, garden, or watch dramatic shows. Sometimes they spend time with societal movements or special causes. They enjoy the finer things in life: sitting in front of a fire with a good novel, soaking in a luxurious bath, listening to excellent music, savoring a box of decadent chocolates, vacationing in an opulent resort, dining in a premier restaurant, strolling through a beautiful and fragrant garden, snuggling with a down-filled comforter, watching a celebrated theatrical production, visiting the museums and monuments of Paris, and so on.

Golds

Golds won't indulge in recreational activities until they've fulfilled all their obligations. Otherwise, they'll suffer so much from feelings of guilt that they become quite miserable to be around. Even when they take time off to rest and recuperate, they don't "cut loose" like their Blue and Orange cousins. Their activities still reflect all their values. They'll do the right thing, in the right way, at the right time, in the right place. Their activities are normally conservative, traditional, and formal. Often, they're ordered towards a specific goal, such as improving family relationships, maintaining health, or entertaining others. Golds usually organize playtime well so that everyone involved understands the expectations, rules, and timeframes. Even though they may appear to be stiff, proper, and constrained, they're experiencing fun in their own way.

Greens

Most Greens appreciate activities that engage the brain in new and intriguing ways. After all, they reason, the greatest adventures in life aren't physical; they're mental. Of course, Greens aren't limited to sedentary cerebral activities; they have their favorite sports and athletic activities as well. In these activities, just like any other Green undertaking, they don't do it just for fun—they do it to acquire competence. So, whether it's pursuing new levels of competence in a familiar field of study, or considering something completely different, Greens are up to the challenge. Just give them enough time and space and they'll amuse themselves forever.

Oranges

Naturally playful, Orange love to have a good time and do all they can to maximize their leisure hours. They are usually involved in a variety of activities, particularly competitive ones, either as a player or an active spectator. They often enjoy physically challenging and daring adventures that take them to new places or allow them to experience new sensations. They prefer to associate with others who are fun or exciting to be with, but don't mind solitary activities that allow them to use their skills. Many Oranges are drawn to any activity that requires at least three *Hail Mary's* before one attempts it for the first time and uses at least two-thirds of the body's available adrenaline.

> "Humanity has advanced, when it has advanced, not because it has been sober, responsible, and cautious, but because it has been playful, rebellious, and immature."
>
> —Tom Robbins

Assignments

- 6A: Make a list of playful activities that would appeal to Blues.

- 6B: Make a list of playful activities that would appeal to Golds.

- 6C: Make a list of playful activities that would appeal to Greens.

- 6D: Make a list of playful activities that would appeal to Oranges.

- 6E: Think of an activity that is normally dull and boring to you. How can you turn it into something that is far more joyful, fun, and enjoyable?

Introduction

How to boost vitality and kill vampires

Some of us believe that vitality belongs to the young—those who are strong, excited, and eager to experience everything that life has to offer. This perception may stem from the seemingly boundless energy and enthusiasm that often characterize youth. However, the question arises: can this quality of vigor and energy be acquired by anyone, regardless of age, health, and circumstances? It's important to challenge the notion that vitality is exclusively reserved for the young, and instead, explore the possibility that it's a state of mind and being that can be cultivated by anyone willing to embrace it.

> Vitality is an approach to life marked by an appreciation for energy, liveliness, and excitement. You have a high need for action, movement, and mobility. You live life as an adventure to be approached whole-heartedly. You are inspired to be enthusiastic, cheerful, happy, and full of spirit.

Vitality sounds wonderful to me, especially as I find myself getting older and experiencing more disintegration and deterioration than I would like. But I'm not going to let my lack of youth ruin my future prospects. This is one virtue that I want to develop quickly—especially since vitality will help propel me through my quest to acquire other valuable virtues.

Here are the six things I've written about vitality that will help us acquire more of this particular virtue. As always, these are simply recommendations and starting points. You will uncover other aspects over time.

First, we're going to start off by taking a measure of our energy. I'll invite you to consider everything you have done and felt over the past couple of weeks and then ask yourself some questions about those activities. Why do you think you lack energy? What are some things that might affect your energy levels?

Next, we will figure out how to boost our energy. I've identified 10 time-tested behaviors that don't require legal or illegal substances to boost your energy. We'll also examine some things we can do to help others who might be suffering from low energy, depression, or a lack of enthusiasm for life.

Next, we will do everything we can to avoid vampires. Of course, we should all avoid the un-dead creatures who feed on our blood, but we should also avoid those who feed off your energy, sap your strength, kill off hope, or replace your positive energy with deadly negative energy. We'll discuss some effective strategies, most of which don't require garlic garlands or wooden stakes.

Next, we will try to regularly demonstrate enthusiasm. That's the intense feeling we experience whenever we are excited or enthralled about something. What excites you? What creates those feelings? How does this relate to temperament? We'll find out.

Next, we will learn how to fire up fascination. We will learn how to channel our inner toddler and allow ourselves to be amazed and absorbed at our wonderful world until we drop from exhaustion. We will learn the important role of surprise, experience, and curiosity.

Finally, we will make time for fun. While we're sitting with each other on the surface of our planet, we might as well have a bit of fun while we're still here. Life isn't meant to be a painful, joyless experience. Of course, what is fun and enjoyable varies for each personality type, so we'll review 50 fun activities for each temperament.

I believe you'll find great satisfaction and enjoyment in developing the virtue of vitality. Embracing this journey has the potential to transform your life, filling it with energy, excitement, and joy. If you don't experience these positive changes, it's possible that you may be approaching the process in a less-than-optimal way. In such cases, let's reevaluate our strategies, explore new approaches, and fine-tune our efforts to cultivate this essential quality. Together, we can create a vibrant and flourishing community, united by our shared pursuit of living life to the fullest.

Lesson 1

Measure your energy

Let's start of by measuring the amount of energy you are currently feeling. Consider everything you have done and felt over the past couple of weeks. Can you answer "yes" to any of these questions?

- Is it sometimes a huge effort to visit with family and friends?
- During meetings, do you get distracted, bored, or have a hard time keeping your eyes open?
- Do you need caffeine or other stimulants to make it through the day?
- Are you eating too much unhealthy food for comfort and pleasure?
- Do you have more headaches than normal?
- Do you find it difficult to get yourself out of bed in the morning?
- Are you seeing more wrinkles, lines, swelling, or droopiness in your face?
- Has it been a few weeks since you last had a good laugh?
- Do you often find yourself getting sick with colds or infections?
- Do you regularly have sore or aching muscles even when you haven't been working out?
- Do you feel more anger or frustration at others than you have in the past?
- Do you feel like you just don't have the energy to make it through the day?
- Do you have a hard time shutting off your thoughts so you can fall asleep?

- Is it difficult for you to accept or handle change?
- Do you dread what might happen in the future?
- Are you feeling fearful, anxious, moody, or depressed?
- Do you wish you could take a nap even though you just woke up a couple of hours earlier?
- Do you have a difficult time remembering details or important information?
- Do you fall asleep as soon as you sit down in a comfortable chair or lie down in bed?
- Have you felt feelings of hopelessness or despair about your situation in life?
- Do you get worked up or impatient about relatively unimportant details?
- Is your decreased desire for sex and intimacy affecting your partner?
- At the end of a day, do you feel like all you can do is sit in front of the TV and zone out?
- Do you have a general lack of enthusiasm for doing anything at all?
- Have you recently experienced muscle weakness, slow reflexes, or imbalances?

While symptoms vary from person-to-person, if you've experienced three or more items from this list, chances are your energy levels are lower than they should be. If this is the case, you feel like you just don't have enough energy and are too tired to accomplish the things you need to do or want to do. You also recognize that it is negatively affecting your life, your work, and your relationships.

To try to fix this problem, some people traipse over to their doctor's office seeking medication to help perk them up. Some quick-fix doctors may prescribe stimulants like amphetamines or methylphenidate to chemically boost their energy; but that often has some nasty side effects which may lead to bigger problems if the drug is used too frequently or for too long. For example, when a person's brain detects the presence of artificial uppers flowing through the body, it stops asking the body to produce its own natural stimulants. Then, when the person stops using the medicine, the person experiences withdrawal symptoms and increased amounts of fatigue. In may take weeks for their body to reset to normal levels.

But most doctors, particularly those who believe in the "do no harm" oath, simply repeat the familiar mantra about getting more exercise, eating healthier foods, avoiding harmful substances, shedding some weight, getting better sleep, reducing stress, blah blah blah. We all know what we should do, we just choose not to do it because we don't like doing it. It is far easier to pop a pill, drink another caffeinated beverage, inhale some nicotine, or score some illicit coke, crack, or crank. But the doctors aren't lying about the health paradox: spending energy to become healthier will give you more energy, as well as more clarity, attention, and alertness.

> "The problem with lethargy is that doing nothing validates the fear that nothing can be done."
>
> —Bill Crawford

Assignments

🖊 **1A:** Even if your personal energy levels are perfectly fine, chances are there is someone in your life who is suffering from low amounts of energy. How is that affecting your relationship?

🖊 **1B:** Do you think people who have a lack of energy are lazy or unindustrious? Explain your answer.

🖊 **1C:** What has caused you to experience a lack of energy in your life?

🖊 **1D:** Some mental disorders list a lack of energy as a symptom. But is lack of energy causing the disorder or is the disorder causing the lack of energy? Explain your reasoning.

🖊 **1E:** Identify some physical diseases or conditions which cause low energy or chronic fatigue.

Lesson 2

Boost your energy

Fortunately, there are many things you can do that don't require legal or illegal substances to boost your energy. Here are 10 effective behaviors.

Eat for nutrition and energy. Rather than eating what is tasty, cheap, comforting, or convenient, regularly consume a variety of nutritious foods that provide complex carbohydrates, proteins, fats, vitamins, minerals, enzymes, and other metabolic nutrients that your body needs for energy. Because people respond differently to foods, and may have allergies or intolerances for certain items, what is healthy for you may be unhealthy for someone else. Furthermore, besides being a highly personal choice based on preferences and tastes, your diet may be limited to what you can afford or what is available in your stores. Higher quality and nutrient-dense foods are often more expensive than low-quality ones, but you should eat as healthily as you can afford. Eating too little food can make you feel lethargic and irritable while consuming too much food will bog you down. Chronic or extreme fatigue and dizziness may indicate a deficiency in certain vitamins or minerals like iron or magnesium.

Increase your movement. If you're physically able, at least 30 minutes of heart-pounding cardiovascular exercise each day will boost your metabolism, increase your stamina, strengthen your heart and vascular system, and improve the delivery of oxygen and nutrients to your body parts—giving you more energy than you expended. If you can't do 30 minutes, at least take a 10-minute brisk walk. This will increase your energy for up to two hours after the walk. Move as often as you can, even while you're sitting behind a desk. Keep moving every day and within two to three weeks, you will see a noticeable improvement in your overall energy levels and mood.

Manufacture more mitochondria. Mitochondria are the power plants of your body. They live within your cells and create fuel from the food you eat and the oxygen you breathe. Having more of them increases your body's energy supply and extends the life of your cells. You can manufacture more of them and make them function better through aerobic exercise as well as eating quality proteins and foods rich in omega-3s and other healthy fats.

Avoid or limit alcohol. While the sugars in alcohol produce some initial stimulant effects at low doses, it is primarily a depressant that slows down your central nervous system, decreases your blood pressure, lowers your heart rate, diminishes your mental clarity, increases drowsiness, and induces relaxation and sedation. Ethanol is addictive and highly toxic.

Stay hydrated. If you're feeling fatigue or lethargic, or your heart is racing for no good reason, it may be a sign that your body is short of water. If you suddenly feel nauseated, start vomiting, or experience bowel issues, you might also have an electrolyte imbalance. If your workout lasts longer than 30 minutes, consider downing a sports drink to bring your salts and minerals back up to snuff. If your urine is clear or straw-colored, you're well hydrated.

Take a short nap. Information overload as well as sustained periods of heavy concentration are physically tiring. A quick nap can reverse those effect and help you retain what you have learned. Naps lasting about a half hour allow you to rest without the risk of entering deep sleep, which may make you feel more tired once you wake up. Skip the nap if you have a difficult time sleeping at night.

Get consistent sleep. Consistent sleep is essential for steady energy levels. Regardless of age, most adults need between 7 and 8 hours of quality sleep each night. Go to bed at regular times, keep your room cool, quiet, and dark, and avoid electronic devices for an hour before going to bed. If you're a snorer, you might want to check to make sure you don't have sleep apnea.

Reduce your burdens. Fatigue is one of the consequences of an over-worked or exploited individual. This isn't just work that relates to your occupation, but housework, homework, and family or social obligations. Whittle down your activities to the "must do today or die" items. When you feel you can handle more, then slowly add back in those that are important, but aren't essential. Leave the non-essentials to the last, delegate them to others, or abandon them entirely.

Reduce stress. Stress is a major cause of low energy and will quickly affect your health and well-being, presenting itself in the form of headaches, digestive problems, acid reflux, asthma, hypertension, skin rashes, and autoimmune disorders. Because each temperament is stressed out by different things, eliminating as many of those stressors is important until you can learn to cope with the strain.

Reach out to others. Regardless of your level of openness or extroversion, external social connections help rekindle our internal fires. They remind us that others are also struggling through tough times. When someone mentions how they overcame their obstacles, it gives us hope for a similar outcome. These interactions also give us warnings about behaviors or situations we may want to avoid. Your social network doesn't have to be broad and expansive to boost your energy—it just needs to be meaningful and strong. When you are tired or feeling low, spend some time with your friends and loved ones to recharge your batteries. Don't be afraid to ask them for help, in fact, they might be offended if they later found out you were struggling and didn't ask them for help.

"People dwell so much on the little things, but why should they hold you back when you have the big things to look forward to? By exuding positive energy when dealing with your problems, you will exude it in your being in general. Treat yourself with love and you will exude love to others."

—Hayley Hasselhoff

Assignments

🖉 2A: What are some additional tips or tricks that you have found that boost your positive energy?

🖉 2B: What can you do to help someone who is suffering from low energy, depression, or a lack of enthusiasm for life?

Lesson 3

Avoid vampires

A vampire is an undead creature who lives by feeding on the vital essence of the living. European folklore suggests that this vital essence is blood, and the best way to obtain it without killing your victim is to sharpen your teeth into fangs and bite someone in the neck, sucking out up to eight cups of blood from the person's jugular vein. But if you really wanted a lot of blood, and didn't care if your victim died, you might bite into an artery which carries the blood directly from the heart, like the radial, femoral, or carotid. It would take less than a minute to gush out about 13–14 cups before the heart stopped beating forever.

While some doubt that blood-sucking vampires exist, you have probably encountered some vampires in your life. But rather than sucking blood, they feed off the energy of others, sapping their strength, sucking them dry, killing off hope, draining people of their vitality. Some perform transfusions, taking your positive energy and replacing it with their negative energy, which can be even more deadly. In either case, wearing cloves of garlic probably won't keep them at bay. And stabbing them in the heart with a wooden stake will likely get you 25 to life in the Big House. About the only thing you can do when you encounter one, is to run in the other direction, alerting anyone in your vicinity to their evil presence.

In all seriousness, there are people who have that effect on others. Some target your emotional energy and feed on your willingness to listen and care for them, leaving you exhausted and overwhelmed afterwards. Others target your intellectual energy, and encourage you to answer questions, solve problems, or create solutions for their benefit—not yours. Some target your spiritual energy, trying to get you to abandon your faith or convictions like they did, because they want you to be miserable too. In every aspect of life, if they see that you have energy in a particularity area, and they don't, they will want to take it from you.

Some energy vampires do this unknowingly, while others do it intentionally. In either case, they are likely to have some of these characteristics:

- Gives ultimatums and reprimands.
- Intimidates or threatens others.
- Passes off sarcasm as humor.
- Avoids taking responsibility for their actions.
- Exploits the weaknesses of others.
- Questions the motives of others.
- Always try to one-up you.
- Complains about every minor issue.
- Seeks power to dominate or control others.
- Easily gets angry or violent.
- Criticizes successful or happy people.
- Creates intricate facades and elaborate deceptions.
- Uses force and compulsion to get their own way.
- Believes they are the center of the universe.
- Ridicules or makes fun of others.
- Highly suspicious of everyone.
- Pretends to be a know-it-all.
- Claims they are regularly victimized.
- Justifies their own negative behaviors.

Whenever you encounter energy vampires in your life, don't underestimate their ability to cause damage. They are masterfully adept at manipulation and will do whatever it takes to come out on top. Don't be tricked into believing you can help them evolve into a better person if you just stick with them for a little longer—they will only change their attitudes and behavior when it is in their best interest to change, not yours.

The only weapon at your disposal is to neutralize their negative energy with your positive energy, and then keep on bombarding them with kindness. Sometimes this works, sometimes it doesn't. But in general, darkness and light cannot exist in the same place at the same time. If you aren't confident in your abilities to kill them with kindness, avoid their sphere of influence. Sadly, some people are like ticking time bombs, sooner or later they will self-destruct and harm everyone within their vicinity.

> "When encountering emotional vampires, see what you can learn. It's your choice. You can simply feel tortured, resentful, impotent. Or, as I try to do, ask yourself, 'How can this interaction help me grow?'"
>
> —Judith Orloff

Assignments

🖉 3A: How can super-agreeable people also drain your energy?

🖉 3B: What can you do to restore your vitality after it has been stolen by an energy vampire?

🖉 3C: What is your plan to deal with the energy vampires who come into your life or the lives of your loved ones?

Lesson 4

Demonstrate enthusiasm

If you have been to a taping of a television show that has a studio audience, like a game show, talk show, or talent show, just before it starts and during commercial breaks, someone comes on stage to stir up the audience and get them excited about what's about to happen. These are called "show warmers" or "warm-up performers" who are paid quite well to animate the audience and get them laughing, engaged, and animated. Like cheerleaders at a sport game, they use whatever talents they have and do whatever they can to create a sense of fun, elicit positive emotions, and encourage an audience to interact through applause, laughter, ovations, and cheers. They do this because they want everyone to have a good experience. Besides, performers genuinely feel and feed off this palpable energy. The more engaged and responsive an audience is, the more engaged and responsive the talent will be. It creates a closed feedback loop where one reaction stimulates another, which stimulates another, and so on. Of course, if the audience responds with boos and jeers, or even dreaded silence, that too has its effect, and the performer will often struggle through their performance even more than their audience.

Enthusiasm is that intense feeling we experience whenever we are excited or enthralled about something. For one reason or another, we sometimes trap that feeling inside and don't let it out. Perhaps it is because we are playing a game of poker and don't want to reveal how we feel about the extremely rare royal flush sitting in our hand. Or perhaps we are so habitually conditioned to not revealing our feelings that we can't help but put a damper on it and remain stone-faced and sober. But hiding these feelings isn't always the best thing to do. In fact, your lack of energy may signal to others that you are not interested at all in the subject, much less enthusiastic about it. It might cost you the opportunity of a lifetime or put the kibosh on a potential new relationship. It might even hurt someone's feelings who thought they were doing something that would get you excited and elicit a positive reaction. In general, unless you are playing poker or intentionally trying to deceive others, don't hesitate to let that enthusiasm out of its bottle and be exhibited through your face, your body, your words, and your actions.

> "Act enthusiastic and you'll be enthusiastic."
>
> —Dale Carnegie

What does enthusiasm look like? Of course, it varies from person-to-person and temperament-to-temperament, but there are still some signs that shout to everyone, "This person is genuinely excited, vibrant, and full of positive energy. I like that. I think I will like this person." Even though you may not be accustomed to showing these reactions to others, it almost always pays dividends. It will lighten the mood, encourage others to engage, endear them to you and vice versa, and enhance your performance. It might take some practice and refinement before these behaviors look and feel authentic, but this type of practice is fun and will always pay off.

- Radiate as much self-confidence as you can muster.
- Keep your energy level higher than those around you.
- Be upbeat, bubbly, reassuring, and cheerful.
- Don't let obstacles and roadblocks get in your way.
- Restate and reinforce the correct ideas of others.

- Be liberal in your praise and compliments.
- Slightly exaggerate your positive emotions to make them obvious.
- Vary your speaking voice by changing the pitch, tone, and volume of your voice.
- Be the person other people want to be with.
- Use friendly and positive hand gestures and motions.
- Demonstrate your sense of humor.
- Make sure people can relate to your message.
- Focus on meaningful benefits.
- Periodically nod your head in approval.
- Use encouraging phrases like, "Tell me more," "Great thought," "Nice insight."
- Look at others as you speak and listen; but don't stare.
- Make your eyes mirror the excitement in your voice.
- Stand up straight with your shoulders back and head up.
- Look like you are enjoying the moment.
- Let your creative juices flower.
- Don't be afraid to stand out from the crowd.
- Move your body more than normal; keep a bounce in your step.
- Neutralize your negative emotions.
- Use facial expressions that show your excitement.
- Act as though you are deep in thought while listening.
- Energetically contribute to conversations.
- Show more positive attitude than those around you.
- Smile with your eyes and eyebrows.

Assignments

- 4A: Why do most employers favor enthusiastic applicants?

- 4B: How can you appear enthusiastic yet maintain a professional demeanor?

- 4C: What are the downsides to having a lot of enthusiasm?

- 4D: Is it possible to learn how to develop and control your enthusiasm, to turn it on when you need it to motivate you to do something you don't want to do? Explain.

- 4E: What is your plan to become intentionally enthusiastic in at least once facet of your life?

Lesson 5

Fire up your fascination

Once upon a time in the far distant past, you were a toddler who was fascinated by absolutely everything in the world. You touched things, looked at it from different angles, investigated its properties, picked it up and dropped it, and maybe even stuck it in your mouth or some other orifice. You did this because you didn't know what it was and what its function would be in your life. Because you didn't understand it, it captured your complete attention. This sense of wonder and fascination compelled you to spend every waking moment totally absorbed in what life had to offer. You had boundless energy until you finally collapsed from sheer exhaustion.

> "Learn how to turn frustration into fascination. You will learn more being fascinated by life than you will by being frustrated by it."
>
> —Jim Rohn

And then you grew up. For at least a dozen years you were taught in schools and through personal experiences how things worked, why they worked, what you should and should not do, and why the world is the way it is. Now, because you possess most of the correct answers to successfully live in the world, you tune out, stop asking questions, and quickly get bored with life and your job and its predictable patterns and routines.

One reason we lack vitality is because we aren't surprised by what life has to offer. That's why we crave surprises, enter contests, participate in challenges, go to casinos, taste new food and drinks, stay up late to watch sporting events and election returns, and are entertained by actors, musicians, magicians, acrobats, contortionists, athletes, celebrities, social media influencers—people who do things that surprise, edify, amaze, empower, or amuse us. It is why we flock to parks, arenas, theaters, cinemas, stores, campgrounds, museums, and stadiums. It is why we read so many books, watch so many movies, and play so many video games. It is why we have a variety of hobbies and fill our lives with different things to do. It is why we move from relationship to relationship, exploring the different gifts people bring to your world. It is why, once we learn how to do a job well, we soon want to move on to something else. We are, regardless of our personality style, curious creatures. When we stop being curious, we get bored, lose our enthusiasm, quench our passions, and our vitality gets flushed down the drain.

One way to rekindle your childlike sense of wonder and increase your thirst for new knowledge and new experiences, is to stop worrying about providing the correct or previously learned response and saying to yourself and others, "I know how that works." Instead, think about all the things you don't know and start asking yourself about those things. Try finding questions to which you don't know the answer. Start saying, "I don't know," more often, and maybe ask someone, "What do you think about this?" You might just learn something fascinating, if not about that object, then about that person.

As your fascination with the world and its occupants increases, so will your attention and energy towards those things. You will have new life, new passion, and new vitality infused into your life. If you aren't genuinely fascinated at something, you aren't trying hard enough. Go back and examine it again, this time, ask yourself questions like these:

- How did it get here?

- What made it possible for this to exist?
- Who was involved in its design, development, or delivery?
- What would happen if this thing didn't exist?
- What other things are like this thing?
- How can it be improved?
- What other uses are there for this thing?
- Can I use this to create something different?
- How can I make a comfortable living that is centered around this thing?
- How can I use this thing to make the world a better place for others?

Assignments

🖉 5A: What are some things you have always wanted to learn more about but haven't yet?

🖉 5B: Practice developing fascination. Think of something that you want to learn more about. Spend at least 15 minutes thinking about it. You can't interact with others or the internet. Ask yourself a variety of what, who, where, and how questions about it. Did it become more fascinating?

🖉 5C: Think about someone who you have found to be fascinating? What triggered your fascination?

🖉 5D: What makes someone fascinating?

🖉 5E: How can increasing your fascination about someone or something give you more vitality?

Lesson 6

Make time for fun

While we're sitting with each other on the surface of our planet, we might as well have a bit of fun while we're still here. Mortality is relatively short and our dream bucket-list of fun things we want to see, do, or experience before we kick the bucket is probably too long, too expensive, and too unrealistic to achieve. But that shouldn't stop us from trying to check off a few of the items from that list. Yes, we all need to work hard, fulfill our obligations, acquire useful knowledge and skills, and try to be better today than we were yesterday, but that doesn't mean we shouldn't take time to have fun with those we care about, and create wonderful, positive memories.

In our final hours of life, most of us won't be fretting over the promotion we never received, or the fame we never achieved, or the bigger house we could never afford, but we will be regretting that we were so caught up with the acquisition of money, power, or prestige, that we didn't spend enough meaningful time with our families, friends, and loved ones. That's part of the reason why we need to intentionally set aside some of the time that we have remaining to having fun with others.

> "If you never did you should. These things are fun and fun is good."
>
> —Dr. Seuss

But there's also another reason. Life isn't meant to be a painful, joyless experience. If we don't offset all the hard work we do with a little play time, we would quickly become grumpy, unhappy, and miserable people. We need to find a balance between work and play that works for us and those we care about. If we don't regularly schedule some leisure time or experience recreational activities, we will quickly burn out or spiral out of control. Fun activities give us a change to recover from our labors, recharge our batteries, work out our tensions, set aside our burdens, discover new things, and enhance our relationships with others.

What is fun and enjoyable varies from person-to-person of course. We certainly see that in the world of temperament, where something that is fun to the Orange would be absolute horrifying to the Gold, Green, and Blue. Below are 200 fun activities that may or may not appeal to you and those around you. Notice that many of them don't require money—they just require time.

200 Fun Activities

- Create something useful.
- Hold a bingo night.
- Reminisce through old photos.
- Visit a formal garden.
- Binge watch an entire season in one setting.
- Help a random person.
- Relax in a hammock.
- Build a sandcastle.
- Throw someone a surprise party.
- Try an unusual recipe.
- Go to a pet show.
- Start a blog or vlog.
- Tour a factory or plant.
- Do something you are afraid of doing.
- Change someone's life for the better.

- Go skating or rollerblading.
- Tie-die a t-shirt.
- Go miniature golfing.
- Hang out with exciting people.
- Dine at a fancy restaurant.
- Watch a play.
- Pull a fun all-nighter.
- Participate in a flash mob.
- Go indoor skydiving.
- Rent a limo.
- Eat something new and unusual.
- Get a couples massage.
- Browse rare books at the library.
- Clean the house—naked.
- Make an origami animal.
- Feed the birds or ducks.
- Volunteer at a charity event.
- Go birdwatching.
- Ride in a hot-air balloon
- Visit an unusual coffee shop.
- Attend an intriguing lecture.
- Take a swimming or lifesaving class.
- Housesit for a friend.
- Go to a wild rock concert.
- Write love letters.
- Pick berries.
- Learn to play a song on an instrument.
- Go beachcombing.

- Recite poetry.
- Complete a massive jigsaw puzzle.
- Go on a double date.
- Go bungee jumping.
- Work on some arts or crafts.
- Sing at a karaoke event.
- Ride a tandem bicycle.
- Visit a corn maze.
- Become a foodie.
- Play tennis, racquetball, pickleball, or badminton.
- Travel around the world—via the internet.
- Try mountain biking.
- Take someone to a museum.
- Participate at an open-mic comedy club.
- Ride all the rides at a carnival or fair.
- Sell something at the flea market.
- Regularly write in a gratitude journal.
- Walk around with a blindfold on.
- Learn to snorkel or scuba dive.
- Swim with the dolphins.
- Stay at a bed and breakfast.
- Audit a random class.
- Build a snow fort.
- Build and fly a kite.
- Go paintballing.
- Learn a new card game.
- Participate in a trivia contest.
- Perform random acts of kindness.

- Walk barefoot on the beach.
- Research family history.
- Pick flowers for someone.
- Go camping.
- Listening to all the music of a composer.
- Learn how to knit or crochet.
- Take a photo in a photo booth.
- Try canoeing, kayaking, or rafting.
- Shop at a farmer's market.
- Visit an amusement park.
- Read some classic literature for fun.
- Try lawn bowling.
- Go snow skiing, snow shoeing, or snowboarding.
- Go to the zoo.
- Grow an herb garden.
- Drive a snowmobile.
- Go to a comic book convention.
- Learn a new language.
- Hike someplace new.
- Cuddle by the fire.
- Learn magic tricks.
- Take a spontaneous weekend trip.
- Have a mini reunion.
- Ditch your phone for a day.
- Kiss in the rain.
- Learn how to tango or waltz.
- Ride a horse.
- Have a water balloon fight.

- Drastically change your hair.
- Have a food fight.
- Discover a new culture.
- Get to your ideal weight.
- Watch a ballet.
- Play in the rain.
- Go hot tub hopping.
- Have a candlelit dinner.
- Gaze at the starry sky.
- Send a message in a bottle.
- Befriend your neighbors.
- Ride in a helicopter or glider.
- Shoot a video.
- Arrange a secret rendezvous.
- Go to an unusual athletic event.
- Make a scrapbook of your favorite memories.
- Learn how to do a flip on a trampoline.
- Participate in a scavenger hunt.
- Play unusual board games.
- Participate in a race or marathon.
- Befriend an elderly person.
- Attend a demolition derby or monster truck rally.
- Repaint your house.
- Paint a picture.
- Go to an escape room.
- Plan an adventure trip.
- Go on a dinner cruise.
- Visit an observatory.

- Pet lonely animals at the petting zoo.
- Build a blanket fort.
- Give out free hugs.
- Race an automobile or motorcycle.
- Exercise with someone.
- Learn something unusual that will make you stand out.
- Learn how to fish.
- Start a new hobby with a friend.
- Go on a scenic drive.
- Learn a foreign language.
- Host a movie night outside.
- Jump in the pool fully clothed.
- Ride on a steam-powered train.
- Act in a play.
- Take someone to a formal dance.
- Get the high score on a video game.
- Jump into a pile of leaves.
- Sign up for yoga.
- Mentor someone.
- Attend the symphony.
- Sleep under the stars.
- Have a romantic picnic at the park.
- Solve a mystery before anyone else.
- Join a sports team.
- Do a cartwheel or handstand.
- Make pottery with someone.
- Play relationship games.
- Learn how to juggle.

- Go to a drive-in movie.
- Shoot some pool with some friends.
- Attend a poetry reading.
- Tour your own city.
- Donate unused clothes.
- Get a makeover.
- Object at a wedding ceremony.
- Gamble away some extra cash.
- Go to a nude beach.
- Drive bumper cars.
- Get a tattoo or body piercing.
- Surf, windsurf, water ski, or wake boarding.
- Go skinny-dipping with a friend.
- Work in someone's garden.
- Go rock climbing or spelunking.
- Solve crossword puzzles in pen.
- March in a parade.
- Play shuffleboard.
- March in a protest.
- Ask someone to dance.
- Adopt a pet.
- Ride a roller coaster 10 times in a row.
- Pick up trash at your local park.
- Give your best friend an unexpected present.
- Name a star.
- Start a side business.
- See your favorite band in concert.
- Join a book club.

- Watch some classic black and white movies.
- Write a song.
- Enter a competition.
- Bit at an auction.
- Take a cooking class.
- Go on a treasure hunt.
- Play a new video game.
- Shop at outlet stores.
- Watch the sunrise and sunset.
- Throw a homemade dessert party.
- Ride in a horse-drawn carriage.
- Invent a new solution to an old problem.
- Go hang gliding or parasailing.
- Learn to use chopsticks with your other hand.
- Crash a wedding.
- Debate and discuss important issues.
- Test drive a sports car.

Assignments

✎ 6A: Make your own bucket list of activities that you can realistically do within the next 12 months. Try to involve others in your activities. Consider their preferences.

✎ 6B: Choose one fun activity that you can do with your friends or loved ones this week.

✎ 6C: What is the minimum and maximum amount of time you will set aside to have fun each week?

www.ingramcontent.com/pod-product-compliance
Lightning Source LLC
Chambersburg PA
CBHW070733230426
43665CB00034B/2000